The Sun and Beyond

The Loving Light Books Series

Also by Liane Rich

Loving Light

Book 4

The Sun and Beyond

Liane Rich

The information contained in this book is not intended as a substitute for professional medical advice. Neither the publisher nor the author is engaged in rendering professional advice to the reader. The remedies and suggestions in this book should not be taken, or construed, as standard medical diagnosis, prescription or treatment. For any medical issue or illness consult a qualified physician.

Loving Light Books
Original Copyright © 1990
Copyright © 2009 Liane

ISBN 13: 978-1-878480-04-0
ISBN 10: 1-878480-04-9

Loving Light Books:
www.lovinglightbooks.com

Also Available at:
Amazon: www.amazon.com
Barnes & Noble: www.barnesandnoble.com

for Elmer

The information in this series is not necessarily meant to be taken literally. It is meant to *shift* your consciousness....

Foreword

Anyone immersed in the vast body of new metaphysical knowledge is aware of the virtual symphony of voices from channeled sources throughout the world – inspirational voices that may be artistic, poetic, philosophical, religious, or scientific. And now, out of these myriad New Age voices, comes a series of books by God, channeled through Liane, revealing the frank truth in all its glory and wonder, telling us how to cleanse our bodies, gain access to our subconscious minds, clear our other selves and march back to who we are – God.

In God's books you will be introduced to a loving, powerful, gripping, exciting, and often humorous voice that reaches out and speaks ever so personally to the individual reader. As the reader's interest deepens, invariably an intimate relationship to this voice develops. It is a relationship that lasts forever, and I am quite certain I do mean forever.

Here is an accelerated program, a no-holds-barred course, where God guides us and loves us, and as needs be recommends books to us and even a movie or musical piece along the way. He (She) enters our lives and sees through our eyes, seeming to enjoy the ride as He guides us back to US, back to ALL. Here is a voice that is playful and informative, that is humorous and serious, that is gentle and powerfully divine. It is a voice that knows no barriers or restrictions, a straightforward and honest voice that caresses us when we need the warmth and pushes us when we are immobilized.

In today's New Age literature there is an avalanche of information from magnificent beings of light, information that possesses us and compels us to look at our fears and express our love. In this series of books by God, you will find truly powerful methods for making this transition from toxicity to purity, from density to light, from fear to love, and from the delusion of death to the awakening to full life. You will experience in these books the love and the power of God for it is your love to express and your power to behold. Rarely will you see more lucid steps for transformation. Read these beautiful words and rejoice in our period of awakening, our return to Home.

John Farrell, PhD., LCSW. – Psychologist, Clinical Social Worker, Senior Clinician Psychiatric Emergency Services, U.C. Davis Medical Center, Sacramento. John is also a retired Professor – California State University, Sacramento, in Health Sciences and Psychology.

The Sun and Beyond

Introduction

In the Beginning I did not wish to contact this girl as she had great fear. Her fears were varied and many. She began to go into her fears and she began to heal her body and she began to write for God. Now you sit with this book and you still do not believe that this girl writes for God. Oh – you have had your moments and even times when you believed in miracles enough to buy some of what I have written in our previous books. But now you sit here and expect me to convince you once again that I am indeed God and that you are on your path to me. So, I will do as you wish and you will wish to know that I will not only convince you once again that I am God, I will also show you who you are, and who you shall be, and where we all come from, and where we are going, and I do love to share yet another book and I am happy to be here.

My pen has been anxious to write and is now very excited that I have awakened her to do so. We have a great deal of work to do once again. We have all done well with our last three books and all is on schedule as planned. We will not be so unkind as to ask you to become God this moment, as there is much work and preparation to be done. Know that I do not wish to condone the use of drugs, and know that I do not condone the use of fear tactics to get others to act as you would wish them. This is not acceptable behavior for God and God does not wish to be involved in such things.

Now, in the beginning I did not communicate with many, as I could not get through the debris you carry in your body. New times are upon us and a new day is dawning, and lo and behold, God is once again walking in human form. Hence we now have the beginning of the Second Coming, and oh, how I love to see this event. So, we will continue our lessons and we will continue to teach love and enlightenment to all who are ready at this time. You all know who I am and you all know who you are. We have all read our first three books, and that information has been received and recorded by the subconscious, and now we are ready for our next step.

Do not believe that you may read this material if you have not first read *God Spoke through Me to Tell You to Speak to Him,* and our second book, *No One Will Listen to God,* and our third book, *You are God.* This is important. No one of you is clear at this time, and the intake and assimilation of material and information in this particular book will cause you discomfort and lack of understanding without the previous information. So, I now suggest that you put this book down or you may find yourself with a large headache after reading its contents. All information must be given to the subconscious mind in a very formative and gentle fashion.

Once again I wish to share my insights, and they are not commonly known nor accepted by those on earth at this time. No one is expected to simply read and accept this information. You will each go through a process of discovery about who you are and how you will work for God. Since we are all God, none of you has a problem with this thought. Know that you will each learn what your purpose on earth is as we continue to transmit the words of God to you through this channel. You often become confused as you read and we are each waiting to guide you inward to your own inner space. We, as you know from our first three books, are the Universal Power of Light, and together with the God force, or as some of you call him, the Akashic Records, we channel through this woman. This seems remarkable to you, but it is not so remarkable. You see – *she is a clear channel* and if you have read our previous books, you know why and how this occurred, and you too are on your path to becoming "clear." So, let's go back to school.

Please turn this page and we will begin. God is back to teach another semester. No more school break. Liane is rested and she is ready and eager to share her writing with you. Go forth and smile and know that I am smiling with you.

God

Now I wish to discuss with you the meaning of Love. You are so confused that you believe love to be something that gets in the way of your having fun. Love is not painful. What is painful is your incessant need to control those you begin to love. Love is not to conquer... love is to surrender. Now, for those of you who have been taught not to give yourselves away, I ask, "Why not?" I don't expect anything of you and I don't change how you act, or speak, or dress, or even feel, and still I love you. I allow you to be exactly who you are, and in doing so, you are able to rise up out of your confusion and begin to love in return. When you begin to love in return, you are loving you as well as me; and in loving you, you begin to have respect for you; and in having respect for you, you begin to share with those that you love; and in sharing, you create gratitude towards those who receive as well as those who have given; and in the gratitude is love and kindness to all.

So, be grateful for any lover who crosses your path at this time. All are teaching you to love, even those who do not appeal to you. You will see you in each and every one who is sent, and when he or she arrives, I do not wish to hear you shout, "Oh no; this is not what I asked for, God. I wanted the tall one, or the rich one, or the kind one, or the generous one, or the one who will send flowers." Give your love to the one who comes asking, as he or she is the one who I have sent, and you will learn most from this person.

Okay, I see that I have begun this book on the wrong note and you are already disinterested in God's information to you. So, let's go to a subject that you will enjoy. This one is you. You all love to talk about you, so let's talk about you. Number one: you *are* number one. Number two: you are not to be so wrapped up in learning to become God that you forget to stop and enjoy being human.

I do not wish any to become so wrapped up in their lessons that they forget to play. Go out and live. Watch the sky change and laugh with the silliness that you have all created for yourselves. Do not expect me to take care of your requests at this time. I am tired of sending your gifts and returning your prayers with answers and you don't listen. And you take one look at my gifts and shout, "Oh no, this one's fat, he can't be mine," or, "Oh no, she has crow's feet, she belongs to someone else." I will tell you now that you will not get to love your perfect mate until you learn to love all.

So, now God has done it. He's asking us to run amuck and love everything that moves. Promiscuity is not bad. Get this nonsense out of your heads. You decided to control your fun or pleasure, as you believed you displeased one another. Suzie and Tommy were having good fun making love, and along comes Gary and says, "Oh no, Suzie, I want you to make love with me, not Tommy," and Tommy laughed; and Suzie said, "I love you too," and Gary said, "No you don't," and Tommy laughed; and Suzie said, "Yes, I do," and Gary got tired of Tommy's laugh and punched him in the nose; and Suzie became upset and blamed herself and now we have guilt. And this guilt is now killing you on the earth.

This guilt has grown to such great proportions that you now die from it and it is called AIDS. Give up guilt concerning your sex lives and AIDS will disappear. No – not you guys; I sit here and watch and wonder how far this will go. And now I see those of you who carry great guilt call it concern for your safety or responsibility to humanity, or just plain good sense to refrain from sex, as "AIDS" is out there. *Guilt* is out there! And now you tell those who are still enjoying sex that they are wrong and you judge them and they are not wrong. They are simply less guilty than you, and now we have quite a mess, don't we? How to know if you carry enough sexual guilt to contract AIDS or draw AIDS to you. Guilt is at the base of all sexually transmitted diseases, and of course a good deal of this guilt is hidden in the subconscious mind and you do not know it even exists. "Who, me, have sexual guilt... no way... I love sex." Don't be so sure, my children.

You have reincarnated many times and not all of you have been able to clear the problems from past life, and so you carry in your subconscious the pain and guilt from other lives. And it compounds and grows and is very big. And now the world is searching for her answers and she is trying to learn to love. And she is going to seminars to learn how man thinks and how woman responds. And she is listening and learning to attract love. And when love comes knocking, she says, "Nope, this one's not for me," and she stumbles on and reads and learns from those who have found their answers. And I send another who can show her where her guilt and fears lie. And she takes one look and says, "Oh no, why do I continue to attract this type?" And I will tell her now. You will always attract like.

You will always draw to you what is most out of balance in you. So you see, these people are my gifts. Take a good look at you in these mirrors. This will do for now. Liane and I have a phone call to make to a certain someone. Good day and welcome to our fourth book, *The Sun and Beyond*. You will all soon be with me, and we will travel to the sun and beyond.

⚜

God does not wish to be with you at this time. He can only be with you when you are in the now and most of you are in tomorrow, or the day after, and even in some cases, next year. So, this is how I wish to bring you into your present. Sit and meditate. Do not confuse this with prayer. Meditation is not prayer. Prayer is asking, or thinking of, and receiving back. Meditation is contemplation without desire. Contemplate on who you are, on how you are connected to this universe and on how you are connected to each other. Do not get in the way of this meditation by directing your thoughts. Allow all thought to flow as has been discussed in our previous three books.

Now is a good time to remind you that you have no business reading this, our fourth book, if you have not yet read books one, two and three. *This is important.* Now, I know how you expect to do as you please, and I know how you believe that you know best for you, and I even know which of you will regard this warning and return to Book One to begin your education. So, don't believe that you are getting away with something simply because you believe yourself to be alone with this book and no one will know. Many are with you and many will know, and you are well aware of this fact if you have read our first three books.

So, now that you are once again *aware* that I watch you, we will continue with those who are ready at this time. Those who are ready know how to begin to meditate as they have been guided to go within by reading our previous material. Now, go to your mate and say, "I love you," and watch as I begin to show you once again how you are all on your path to your twin soul, or the other half of you. We left off in Book Three with each of you putting your best foot forward to dress *your* best for your twin, and with you clearing debris from your body in order to release old programming that keeps you from your twin, and even with you learning to love your twin unconditionally. And now you are back to learn what to do now.

So, you of the Universal Power of Light do not wish to communicate with those who are of this earth at this time. Now, I see you are confused. This simply means that you do not wish to be a part of the 'you' that is in body. You have guided from outside of body for such a long time that it is considered painful to return. I am requesting that you go into body and reside and guide as I have with this girl. You will find little discomfort, as a good deal of change has begun to take place and the body is being prepared by the will.

So now you see the problem. I, God, must contact *all* parts of you, and in so doing, I put you in touch with the rest of you, and in so doing, you begin to learn that there is more to you than body. So now you are all certain that I know how you created this body, as we went into this in great detail in our previous books. So, I will start where we are now. No going over old material. If you have forgotten your lessons, I wish you to reread our first three books and come back to this book when you have finished.

So, you now live *in* body. *You are not body.* You are spirit and soul and energy and essence and love and many, many others that you may never know. We have an angelic you, and an astral you, and a spirit you, and a mental you, and even an alien you, and many past you's. And they each have their spirit, and their angel and their alien. And we have parallel you's, and they co-exist with you right here on earth on another dimension. And they are all learning to live in matter as you are, and they are the you's that affect you most right now.

You see, these parallel you's travel alongside you and begin to bump into you from time to time. This is due in part to the fact that they are direct thought energy and have a strong draw to you. See; you send out new you's without your knowledge. You must be pretty good at this creating business to be able to project new you's into other universes and times without your own knowledge.

So now we have you wondering how this can be and I will explain. You do not always know what choice to make in life so you contemplate and dwell on what decision you will make and what course of action to take. And eventually this thought power that you are generating becomes so strong that you are now projecting an image of you in another time and space. Say you are contemplating marriage; "Should I ask her, should I play it safe and stay single?" You envision you married to her and her responses and reactions to you and then you envision you single and having a good ol' time. And then the day of decision comes and you decide to go for it and jump into matrimony.

So now we have this you who lives on this planet and you are a happy man about to propose. And your thought energy on this subject is so powerful that it has taken *form* in another dimension. And now we have a you in another dimension who is already married and living with her; and we have the other side of your thought pattern, which is a you who is miserable and lonely, but he has his freedom; and he is struggling to know himself better, and he is single and thought by most to be having a good ol' time.

You have just created two more of you and each of

them is you and each of them reports back to you, and each of them affects this particular life and each and every decision you make in this life. And their effect on you is based on their own needs and desires and knowledge of what is. And their basic knowledge of what is has come from you, as you are their master. You are the big head honcho – the guy who created them. And they look to you for guidance and you don't even know that they exist, so every now and then they come back to nag at your mind and remind you who you are, or how big you really are. And you can bet that every major decision in your life has created more of you, and now you begin to see how vast and yet small and insignificant you really are.

You are like a big computer who is spewing out replicas of himself, and you are only a machine and you don't know how to stop, or change what you are doing, as you have been programmed. And now your memory banks are reprogramming from old programming. And this computer has turned into a monster who kills, because of old stuff that was once programmed by an old part of the machine itself when something went haywire. Only the computer does not know he went haywire and now he spews out new computers with old haywire information. And so the new computers continue this process of believing they are doing good when it is not good, it is simply misinformation that got into this system.

And I am God, and I am the master computer of all, and I wish to inform all my computers that we are now being reprogrammed, and it is very important to reprogram in the same way we became programmed or we will short circuit and shut down. Do not read this book until you have read our first three books or you may become short circuited and of no help to us at this time. We wish all of you in all dimensions to clean out your memory banks and begin again with correct programming, and this *is* possible and we will all learn to do this process.

So for now, I will wish you a very good day and allow Liane to realize what I have just channeled through her body. She believes that I am God and now she wonders just who God is.

⚜

Now I will tell you another story. This time I will tell you about Tommy. Once upon a time Tommy began to learn about God and this universe and Tommy did not wish to be part of this universe, he wished to escape to other planes and dimensions. And now we find Tommy working in other realms and asking why he has not yet become God and why he does not yet "feel" like God and God will now tell him.

You do not get to God through a mental or physical process. You get to God through the emotions. Love is the most powerful of these emotions and in loving yourself unconditionally, you are loving your twin soul, and your twin soul is you and he/she will return to you when you are good enough to you. So, do not worry that you lose in this game of God. No one loses. No one comes out on the short end of the stick. No one gets left out or left behind. We will all find love. Each and every one of you who are on planet earth at this time will discover love. Not true love, as there is no such thing. What you will discover is real love. Your own love is at the base of all that you are and all that you are is love. So, you cannot 'not' love. It is impossible. When you stop judging, you will fall in love because without love you simply do not exist.

Now, I wish to explain for you that you will not always know love, as you have become so confused and surrounded by debris that you do not "feel" what you are and you do not know that what you are is love, or God. So, we come back to this simple task of being exactly who we are and letting our light shine and showing our "true colors" to all. And how do you do this? Be you. Do not force you on others, especially if this new you does not co-exist well with their feelings and beliefs. But nevertheless, be who you are. Show all how to be exactly who they are. This will not be so difficult as you believe. Allow all to be exactly who they are and all will go well. Do not argue or try to convince anyone of your point of view.

So now you have the ticket out of confusion and into love. Be and let be. Live and let live – two very good mottos to live by. So, I ask you each to be and live and allow others to be and live. And soon you will all be running around feeling very good about who you are, and you will not wish any to be left out of your love. And soon you will be so happy with you that you will be crazy about, and in love with, yourself. And this will mean that you are crazy about, and in love with, *all* parts of you. And since your twin is you, he or she will feel this love and be drawn to you, and now we have you in love at last and knowing exactly who you are, and this love vibration continues to draw all parts of you back to God. And before you know it we have our centipede waking up to the fact that it is all his body that covers this earth, and in his awakening comes our salvation and the salvation of this planet.

So you see; you do count. You are each part of the whole, and who is to say that a finger or toe is not as important as an arm or a leg, and we all want to become whole and healthy again, and I will show you how this will be done soon. So now you have a good deal to work on for tomorrow's class. Love you by allowing you to be you and love all by allowing them to be them.

⬥

*O*nce you begin to realize how you are each part of a whole, you will begin to give up on struggling and warring and fighting with your neighbor and the ones you love. You are all part of this big system and you all begin to grow and outweigh your own beginnings with thoughts of how big you should become in the eyes of others, or how sophisticated you should look to those you admire.

I am now going to tell you a story. No one of you is perfect. You may see your neighbor as less than you but he is not. Each and every one of you is to come back to me. So, give up this quest to become better than, or more important than, or even to just look good to others. So often you do not accept my gifts because you see you as taking a step down by accepting this job or that job, or dating this person or that person. There are no steps down. All ways to God lead up and now you will feel better about dating that special someone who has your attention, but he just doesn't fit in and what would your friends say? Or, "Oh no, what if my friends were to learn that I now clean houses for others and actually enjoy it when they know how accomplished and accepted I once was?" Do not live your life for others. Begin to live for you. You are the best when you are doing what you really "feel" like doing.

If you love someone who is not accepted by your friends, do not ask them to accept that person. Live and love for you. You are the only one who matters and in giving your friends a say in your relationships, you are giving them your power, and they will begin to take that power and tell you exactly what you most fear hearing. *Don't ask.* Live by your own rules and love by your own rules. Love them all, absolutely everyone who walks across your path and know that they are my gifts to you. Happy loving and happy living your own lives.

You do not at this time wish to become one with your twin as you do not feel that he or she is accepting you. You believe that they reject you and you believe that you must be kind and understanding and forgiving and even the one who apologizes. So now I will tell you how you may get what you desire, which is a better response from your lover. Do not be so sure that this is not a topic for God to discuss as I believe I wish to discuss all areas of your lives and even your non-lives. So – back to the reluctant lover. Do not be so unkind as to point out their shortcomings to them. Love them and watch them grow. You see, they will respond to love. UNCONDITIONAL LOVE is the answer. No restrictions, no requirements, no discussions on how things might be better. Just sweet love and understanding without a hint of criticism and judgment.

Casual comments are a very poor example of corrective advice. Many of you continually drop hints about the areas you wish to see changed in your twin's personality and I will tell you now that you will receive the greatest benefits by not suggesting changes. Only love and respect and *allow them to be* exactly who they are. "How does this teach them?" – you ask. They will admire you so much that they will begin to imitate your behavior, and now you will have anything you wish. Simply be and do and love and soon your twin will catch on and be and do and love just as you do.

So now I wish to thank Liane for this opportunity to share my insights on this subject and allow her time to rest. She has once again become overzealous in her desire to write for God and she will be of no use to me if she does not slow down and recharge her batteries. Good day to you all.

∾❦∽

So now you know how to draw your twin to you and I will wish to keep you informed as to how to keep them, and by the time you finish this series of books you will be drawing and loving and accepting all as part of this lesson.

So let's move on to who you are. You are not who you believe. You are not human and you are not body, and you are not to become so concerned with life on earth that you forget where you have been and where you are going.

In the beginning you did not wish to create out of matter, and you did not wish to love one another, and you did not wish to be here on earth. You each began this experiment to see how you could learn more about who you are, and you became so involved in this test that you do not now remember your true beginnings. Now you are in a position to become one once again and you do not wish to learn who you are. You have lasted this long as you have been guided by others and held in place in this universe long enough to allow you time to come to terms with the facts of your stability. So now you do not feel as though you are of any importance and you do not see your relationship to this universe, and you are only now beginning to rise up and walk with insight into the possibility of the vastness that is you.

You are so stuck in matter that you have forgotten your mission to earth. You do not spend time here out of punishment nor do you spend time here out of social recreation. You spend time on earth to learn to grow. You got mixed up and became stuck in matter and it became important to allow you to return to earth to conquer your fears. Your fears allowed you to get stuck. You did not come to earth to play and become angelic beings of matter. You once came to earth to expand *as* matter and when "the fall" occurred you were so frightened by the fears you created that you did not fight to rise up. So now you return and reincarnate and you do not do so to learn to become a perfect praying saint. You do so to learn to conquer your fears.

So, go out and stop this nonsense about being good and begin to be God. *God is love.* He does not cower in a corner in fear that he will not go to heaven if he displeases his father. He does not judge others as not good enough, especially those who are taking chances and going "out on a limb." God does not wish you to honor, or defend, or worship fear in any way. Fear is not your true God. Love is your true God. So now you know.

You will wish to begin to let go of fear at the moment you finish reading this. This is important. *No fear is to come home to God.* We do not wish to mix darkness with light as it is impossible. The two do not co-exist. So now you see where we get the story of heaven and hell and even purgatory. Fear is dark and darkness creates confusion. *Hell is confusion.* Love is light and light creates awareness. Heaven is awareness, and when you are half-way, you are working from awareness at times and confusion at times, and this is the half-way point. You are now in purgatory.

You do not "know" how to continue on to heaven, or awareness; and so God is intervening at this time, and sending you help, and giving you guidance, and speaking to you for the first time in a very long time....

❧

Once upon a time you did not wish to be the only soul to inhabit form and you asked that you become one with all. You do not inhabit form. You simply exist in it. You not only do not inhabit it, you will not stay in. So now you are confused and I will explain. *You do not live in the body.* You have begun to leave the body and you return at brief intervals and you do not find it comfortable to stay. And now we find you gallivanting around this universe in search of an easier way and all this gallivanting has led you to many who are now assisting in this project.

So, you will learn to stay "in" when you learn to clean house. You do not stay in the body as it is full of dark energy that is deadly. This dark energy has a life force of its own and is killing you. This life force energy that is killing you is fear. Fear is not evil, it is simply darkness and now it is time to *turn on* the light.

You walk this planet and you do not know how you got here and you no longer wish to remain. You see; you accepted this job. You volunteered. You came to earth of your own accord and on your own advice and now you cry that you do not like this work. It is too difficult and now you want out. You do not get out this way. I will not allow you to give up on you, for if I do I am allowing a part of me to be put to sleep, or death, or unconsciousness.

You are not the only life force who is involved. There are a great many others who wish to be out, or gone, or return to safety. Fear has begun to take over to the extent that you no longer believe yourself to be God. So now you wish to run and hide as you once did in the Garden of Eden and this will not be allowed. *You are God.* Do not pretend to be man or any other form. You are God. Become God. Trust you and you trust God. Know you and you know God. Do not get so wrapped up in life that you forget to live. Do not become so accustom to pain and discomfort and illness and disease that you allow it control.

You are slowly giving up and walking away. I want you to come back and take a stand. Come back to God. Do not stray further into darkness and fear. In running, you do just that. You walk away from love. You have spent your life walking away from love. Give love a chance. Say I love you and act like you do until you actually feel love once again. Don't be so silly as to allow this ego to take over. This ego is out of sync with God and is destroying God. This is not good to see and I want to stop this nonsense before you create greater darkness.

The darkness on this planet is so severe that it has extended to the sun and beyond. And now you have a sun who reflects your death right back to you and you believe your God to be harmful, and you see this sun as a danger and she is not. She is your heart; your love source; the food for nurturing. The heart of God is sun. The mind of God is moon and the earth is mother. Stop blaming the heart for not loving and nurturing. She is simply showing you 'you.' Your reflection is now being sent down to earth on the rays of the sun, and you shout to cover your eyes and protect your skin, and it is all your negativity coming right back to you.

You do not run this universe. You have lost control. You sit and wait to see how all will be saved by others and I will tell you now that you will be the savior of you. Come down off the cross. This crucifixion has gone on long enough. Be love and light and you will begin to project love and light, and you will receive love and light.

Now, I wish to explain that you are not to fear this information. Learn by it and project only goodness and love and this is what your mirror will reflect. You are not in danger. You are being warned. The road is unsafe up ahead and many are warning you so you may take an alternate route. Go to those you love and ask them to love everyone, and soon everyone will receive love in return, and everyone will be very happy and love God, as everyone is God, and when everyone loves God we will be saved.

So now you see the big job we have ahead of us. Not only do you not know who you are and what you are doing on earth, you do not know how you are reacting to who you are. You cry and whimper and at times even beg to be out of these situations you have created for yourselves, and you do not realize on a conscious level that you do this. You believe you are living and enjoying life, or, in some cases, living and struggling through life. You do not realize how important it is to communicate with *all* of you.

Now we will take a good look at some other parts of you who are very upset with this conscious you. You will find that this imbalance is centered in the will, and that in communicating with the will, you will begin to balance, especially in the emotional sense. The will controls the body at this time and it is necessary to return to a balance within the body and let the will take some time off. You all are trained to use your will-power to do whatever is most difficult for you to achieve, and in doing so you are activating the power, and it is building and taking over.

So now we may have 'body' who says, "I wish to rest today as my muscles are torn and exhausted." And 'will' is in charge of delivering this message to the correct source in the brain. And instead of listening to 'body,' 'will' decides he knows best, as he is working now from strong desire motivated by ego, and now we have imbalance and disharmony. 'Body' is screaming to rest and 'ego' is screaming for perfection. And 'ego' does not agree that God is perfect, and so 'ego' and 'will' control mind and drive 'body' on. And soon 'body' tears a ligament or has a damaged knee (as we all know the ego rides in the knee) and now we have injured 'body' simply because the emotions of 'body' were ignored.

Do not ignore any part of you. You were created out of perfect harmony and balance. Do not interfere in your own perfection. This system works. Leave well enough alone. Listen to your own good advice. Do not run and jump when your body is fighting it. It fights for good reason. Its job is to repair and rebuild and you are forcing it to do what is not good for it and you are ignoring it and it is unhappy. 'Body' has not been listened to in years.

Now, I do not wish those of you who have abused your body by overeating to sit there and say, "Oh good, here's my way out. God is saying do not exercise." God is not saying, "Do not exercise." He is saying, "Listen to body." So, you must learn to listen also. When 'body' wants to stop eating... stop! You sit and shovel food into 'body' until he can no longer function properly and he begins to break down, one cell at a time. Then you lie down or sit down and he chokes on his own body elements and it is not possible for him to digest the overstuffing and chemicals. And since most of you who are fat belong in exercise, I wish you would listen and get up off your chairs and walk. Walk in the outdoors and communicate with nature as you once did. Turn off your television and begin to live again.

So now I see that I have upset you by calling you fat. You are not to be so displeased with this word. Fat is simply a condition as is skinny or large or lean or tall or short. And fat is a good one to have as it is easily changed, and we will work with you on this. Here we go with a new lesson. God is now teaching diet tricks. Most of you who stuff your bodies do so out of great guilt. Get your mind off guilt. Go to a hypnotherapist or a psychiatrist and ask him to discover where your guilt lies. The therapy may take time but the rewards are worth it.

Everything is connected. No part of you is in this alone. All emotions are centered in this debris that is wreaking havoc in the body. No disease is caused by debris alone. The debris simply stops in the area that is already weak. Weak ego – weak knees. Weak derriere – weak power. Weak financial security – weak back. But you already know this as you have all purchased *You Can Heal Your Life* by Louise Hay, as one of your school textbooks.

So, the symptoms go on and on and are as varied as you are, and when you begin to receive a symptom from your body you pop a pill to shut it up. Stop popping pills for every problem in your life. You are shutting down your body's only communication with you. Your body sends a signal to say, "I hurt, we need help in this area," and you shove down a pill and believe you have fixed everything. Then your body must find a new signal, or code, to send out to get your attention so you will help, and he is again shut up with a pill.

And now here we are and our body is giving up and

dying. He has sent signals, and sent signals, and sent signals, and no one listened, and the doctor wished to cut the bad stuff out of the body, but the emotional stuff was still in the subconscious mind and grew into another symptom and killed the body anyway. So, we will wish to take a look at this system of communication from our body, and begin to listen to our body and look up our symptom in *You Can heal Your Life*, and begin to speak to our soul and ask how this one can be solved. And he will guide you.

As in the case of my pen, some will have what they believe to be big traumas that are buried deep within the subconscious. In these cases hypnotic therapy is best and is not so expensive as other forms of healing. Just imagine, in one sitting you too may know why you have always battled food, and in this knowing, you will begin to grow in awareness and enlightenment as to how this has run your life. And in this enlightenment you will see your lesson as not so traumatic after all. And then we see you begin to change your eating habits, all because you took the time to listen to your body and his signals.

So, go to your friends and ask them to guide you to a good therapist and we will all feel better, and when you see him please ask him to question your subconscious about guilt and anger. Tell him you wish to learn why you are guilty, and angry, and see where these problems lie, and he will help as he will know that you already know that you are the problem; not others, but you.

In taking responsibility for you, you are taking responsibility for all. For in you clearing you, you clear *all* you's. Now go and enjoy this session. If you should go to a very enlightened soul you may wish to ask him also to show you the future under hypnosis. This is easily done as many are now hypnotizing others and showing them past lives. You may also look into your future and this may be most enjoyable for you. So, know who you are... all of you, and know and listen to your body, and know and listen to the messages it sends, and go get fixed. We want you all to be in tip top shape for this Second Coming; no more death and no more destruction. It is simply not necessary. Go in peace and God bless you.

You do not believe yourselves to be so important as God. *You are God.* You do not wish to be called God and you do not wish to take responsibility for being God. You see; if you *are* God then you did all this. You created it all. You left your home and went to earth and created all the messes you now see, only you did not intend to do so. So now you sit and wonder how God can create messes and even how God can survive in all this darkness, and I will now explain.

You do not take the time to think good thoughts, and in doing so, create a good world. You sit and dwell on negative thoughts until negative becomes reality and positive becomes a thing of the past. You once believed in miracles and you created miracles. You now believe miracles to be tricks created in the minds of others. Look at this book and the three before this. You hold a miracle. Do not believe that this is simply explained away. Many will try and many will criticize and even judge this woman as doing evil. *She does not do wrong.*

She has such a strong belief in fairy tales and miracles that she created one for you all. And now you hold these books and you just know that there must be a practical explanation for all this, and it must have to do with the mind. And I will tell you now that she is creating miracles in place of negative thought, or even what you would call ordinary thought.

You begin to believe strongly enough, and the thought pattern lodges in the mind, and the mind takes over and creates examples by which your beliefs might be acceptable. And this information is then stored for you in the mental storeroom of the mind. And whenever you see someone try to talk you out of your beliefs, your mind reminds you that you have proof of what you believe and so you tell them they are wrong. *No one is wrong… ever.* This is due to the fact that each and every one of you is learning a different lesson based on how high you have risen in consciousness and how much you wish to learn this lifetime.

So you now have you believing in miracles and along come all those rational thinkers and they convince you that miracles do not exist. But your mother said they did and you saw miracles every day when you were very small. And since your job in this life is to write books for

God you carefully registered all information concerning miracles. And every time Mom said, "*You can* do this, as anything in life is possible," you reaffirmed your belief in miracles. And now you are an adult and others say, "You can't do it this way, you sound like a crazy person and you will not be accepted," and your mind says, "No, this is right. I know it's right. I was taught how to do this." And so you continue and you allow all who think you are crazy to fall by the wayside as you know that their thought patterns are simply different.

And now you see how you too may create miracles in your lives. Many of you *know* as you read this material that you have a bigger job to do and you know that you too can create miracles. Some of you will do more practical work for God. Do not believe that miracles are better than practicality. I do not judge any for the lessons they have chosen. You picked your jobs. You were not selected because of your talents. You each possess all the same attributes and qualities, only now you show those you have practiced and you do not show those you are working on, out of your own need to evolve. If you do not have patience it is only because *you* chose to come into this life without it so you could learn to develop it. If you do not know how to share, it is simply you teaching you to share. If you are writing books for God it is you teaching you the power of prayer, and if you are a scientist for God it is you teaching you the power of practical thinking.

Liane prayed to me each night and asked me to intervene in her life – to show her a better way. She did not ask for specifics as she had given up on asking for what she wanted. She had received what she had requested in this life and what she received was not what she really wanted. And she knew she did not know how to get love back into her life, so she turned to God and said, "I quit. I give up. Teach me love. Show me how you want me to be. Show me how to do your work. I will do whatever you ask... just show me." And she meant it and I showed her, and here she is two years later and doing my work and giving up all she once knew. And yes she has created a lonely path for herself in that many who once knew her find her out of sync with what they believe is normal.

So now you know. No one gave you a job that is beneath you. You chose long before you came to earth and now you worry that you do not have a purpose. And I will tell you now that if you sit with this book in your hand, you are on your path back to me, and you are being guided to your right place, and soon you will know where you chose to be.

So, go to those you love and tell them how happy you are to know them as you know that they have a special purpose in this life, as you do. We all have our own job to do and it's a very special job for us or we would not have selected it. This is good for now. Go to those you love and tell them that miracles really do exist. You know because you have seen one.

❦

*I*n the beginning you believed you did not belong in body, as body began to break down. You began to leave for brief periods of time and you began to take spirit with you. You did not return to body out of desire, but rather out of the will to keep body. You have now come to a time in your history when you will wish to go back into body. You are walking outside of you. You are guiding from above this body of yours. This is how you will do from now on. You will return to body and move into body and begin to take control of body once again. You have given up control and your body has been taken over by others of you; ego you; will you; subconscious you; even death you.

So now you are confused as is expected and I will explain. You are not you. You believe you are body and soul and that you exist in body and soul, but you are not in body. The soul is out. The soul has split – left town – run out – gone for the day. So now I write this to you as to communicate to soul and allow soul to *realize* that he is best off to return. Soul does not know he is outside body. I know this is confusing to you, especially since I have told you that we write this to you; God and all souls of this galaxy and beyond. I will explain for you as well as I can at this time. You are scattered and I am communicating to all parts who will listen. You – meaning *all* you's; astral, spiritual, mental, physical, supernatural, and so on.

So, you do not know that you are not in your right place. Your soul has agreed to write this information without knowledge of the fact that he is misplaced. He believes he is in his right place and you keep him at a distance and out of body. He does not realize that it is his job to return to body. He has hopes that you will do the work by communicating with him. In communicating you allow him to guide and you allow him some control in your life.

Liane once wrote for her soul, and she most enjoyed his counsel and advice. She now believes he has returned to God which he has. You see; he is the part of her who has returned to allow the connection possible to write these books. He is connected to God and connected *in* Liane, and now she is a giant extension cord from heaven to earth, and the energy travels through her soul and out her hand, and this will not show you how I do this work so don't even try to figure it out.

Now – back to your soul who writes this book with me. Your soul, as explained in *God Spoke through Me to Tell You to Speak to Him*, is continuing to guide from outside your body. He has been asked if he will return to body and at your request he will. He is now asking you to invite him back as you read in our very first book. So now he is writing with me as Liane writes with me. Her soul is part of these writings as is yours, and in the same way that Liane writes through her soul, you may write through your soul.

Now, when your soul was asked to return he did not enjoy this idea and is still not crazy about it. Many of you at one time in Atlantis and Lemuria communicated with your souls quite frequently, and your soul guided and often times was told to keep his big nose out of your business. Since most of you still hear a little voice that you sometimes call "conscience" you may remember. At times your soul would sound off like this little voice of conscience and you would say, "Shut up, I'm having fun and I don't need you to spoil my good time." You see; Atlantis and Lemuria were some pretty wild times in your history. So now you are telling this soul voice to keep his nose out of your good times and he finally says, "Okay, fine, I give up on you," and he did. He left.

There was once a perfect balance within body, and all aspects of you had a specific job to do. But once "the fall" occurred you began to short circuit, go haywire, reject other parts of yourself. You have rejected your souls to the point that they are outside of your body and they hover and guide as they often do at birth. Soul does not always enter in the womb and will guide from outside the form until it feels good to enter. Once he has entered he is very cautious about how he guides as he knows he will be sent packing at the least little indiscretion. And often this occurs about puberty, or sometimes nine, or ten years of age, and "Oh boy" do you have a good time then. So, now we have all these souls who are offering to return, however they do not wish to be in pain and darkness and confusion, and they will wish to guide you to clear this debris you carry in order to communicate freely with you. Hence... enema.

Enema will clear this debris and dark energy and allow you to communicate with your own soul. And your soul will allow you to apologize for past misconduct on your part. And past misconduct may be let go of as simply another lesson, and both you and soul will begin a new relationship. You are gradually cutting off your arms and legs to spite yourself. You stop parts of you from functioning out of distaste of the lessons that you yourself chose to learn on earth. When the going gets tough you get rid of the parts of you who tell you to go into your fears, and so they shut up, or leave all together. And now you sit confused and mixed up and sick and tired – tired of this struggle called life. You are creating this struggle. Give up. Let go and let God. "Trust me." I am not selling used cars. I *am* selling perfect balance and harmony and peace and faith and love… trust me. *I am God. I am* your father. The one you all came from and will return to.

Now, back to this writing. I do not do this writing for you alone. I do this writing for your soul, as he does not know or realize that he does not wish to return to body. He believes he is set to go at your invitation, and I wish him to know that he is not and will try to discourage himself, as he carries old memories of past injustices just as you do. You will each wish to return to one another and I will have peace within my kingdom.

You see; in order to put me back together again I must first put *all parts* of me together, and then the whole will automatically fall into place. Put you together as a perfect functioning body, soul, and mind, then put this perfect you together with your perfect twin. Then march the two of you back to me. And I will have millions of twins coming home and I will come together quite quickly. And we will draw others as we go, and the light will burn bright and draw other light just like moths to a bulb.

So now you know. You are scattered, and not all parts of you know who the rest of you might be, and not all parts of you know your answers, and so I will continue to speak to you separately until you come together as one. This will do for now. Be love, be light and be you... whole... all of you.

❧

You do not believe that I am God and once again I will give you what you require to show you who I am. So, here I go with another story. This time I will tell you about our Bible. I wrote the Bible through many and I did not do it as I do these books. At the time the Bible was transcribed it was a very big job. So many were involved that I do believe it contains the beliefs of everyone who was involved or even concerned at that time with Christ's teachings.

So, now I have all these wonderful volunteers who are putting down in writing what Christ taught, and of course they write it as they see it, and then they add their own information and beliefs as well. And now you have the beliefs and teachings of many in one big book. And of course, the teaching technique at this time was word of mouth and, oh boy, do you on earth love to embellish and change things to make it sound right or more impressive. And you add words and you subtract words and now we have a whole new meaning to what was taught by Christ. Take a small group of people and tell them a story. Make it a short story and then ask each of them to write this story down a week later. Then meet with them again and listen to all the varied versions of this one story. There you have it. Confusion creates confusion.

So many parts of this holy book were never put down as taught. And now this book has been rewritten and revised and rearranged so many times that it is not at all what Christ taught. Very little of what is in your Bible today are Christ's teachings or even the Apostles teachings. It's all been lost in the translation. And now you form study groups to try to make sense of it and it is a waste of time, as your teachers place their own translations on it and now we have more translations. Read this Bible if you wish to but do not live by it. Give up the Bible. It is not necessary to clutch and cling to the teachings of others when you are God and you have all the same information at your fingertips.

Now you know and I do hope that those who hold on to these teachings as law will relax a little and give the rest of my children a break. This nonsense of shouting and screaming hell and damnation has gone far enough and I wish it to end. You will never find in the Bible or anywhere else outside of you your answers. Be gentle and loving and kind in your teaching methods. Christ spoke softly and carried great impact and he did not use a book. He told stories. Now I will tell you my pen's favorite story. This story has given her the strength and courage that she required to be different or strange. Such stories were often told by Christ but not meant to be taken literally.

"Once upon a time there lived a wonderful king. He loved his people and was so beloved by them that his birthday was a holiday within his kingdom. This king lived on a hill above his village that he ruled and he often went down into the village to visit. The water source for this village became poisoned one day, and since the villagers all use the well in the center of the village, all were affected by this tainted water, and all lost their senses and went a little crazy.

So one afternoon the king decides to go visit his people, and when he arrives in the village he sees them all running around acting and talking crazy. He is worried and perplexed. What could be wrong with his beloved subjects? He returns to his castle to think. Later in the day he decides to check once again in the village. Same situation; they're all crazy and running amuck. It's a very hot afternoon so he stops at the well for a drink of water to cool himself. That evening there is a big party. A huge celebration is given by the villagers because their king, just that afternoon, regained his sanity and became one of them once again. The end."

So, who is crazy, them or you? Don't buy into what they are telling you about your strangeness in being on your path to God. Listen only to you; your own voice; your own guidance. They may be drinking tainted water.

Now, some of you may repeat this story to your friends and see how many change the original version. Others may wish to translate this to mean that you should never share drink or food with commoners. Still others may translate this story to be saying that you must keep a distance from those who are crazy or you will go crazy. Do you see how you translate and change things?

And now we have this Bible that everyone is screaming about and you put your faith in this book instead of in yourself. Your faith is misplaced. Put your faith back where it belongs. This is not meant to take your Bible from you. Read it, enjoy it, and know that there is good information in it as well as misinformation.

So, here I go once again upsetting the clergy and those of you who make your living translating the bible. I do not wish to put you out of work so I will ask you to teach new laws; new rules. Number one rule is to love yourself unconditionally, for in loving you, you love all, as you are all. Number two rule is to love all who come into your life as you love yourself, because they are yourself, and number three rule is to let go of fear. Trust and faith without fear; do not fear being alone in all of this. You will soon draw many new friends who will be in the same place that you are and they will love you even though you "look" like the crazy one.

Crazy is all in the eye of the viewer. You were once thought to be crazy for wishing to fly. Now you fly hundreds at one time. Man once thought the world to be flat and when this guy named Columbus said differently, the information was at first disregarded simply because it "seemed" too crazy. This guy called Einstein was really a wacko in his time, but look at the respect and admiration he receives now. And then there's Edison... a light that switches on... he must be out of his mind! And on and on it goes, down through history.

You are not victims who are being punished for being different. There are no victims. You chose to learn to be leaders and here you are learning to lead and it gets a little tough so you run and hide as my pen does. She will learn as you will learn. You have too little faith and too much fear children. Let go of this hold on fear.

Once again I will become repetitive and tell you just who writes this book. Do not accuse this girl of slandering your Bible. She has not read the book and knows very little about it and does not care one way or the other if you believe in it or not. She owns her own Bible and it makes her feel good to do so. She did not write this to you, I did, and if you take the time to communicate with me and my angels we will explain for you. So, do not judge her for these writings. She is simply the pen and she does not wish to answer for her boss and his actions. She only works for me... she is not me. She is, however, you and you are me. You explain that one and you will know a great deal more than either of us.

～♨～

You do not wish to hear me tell you stories about you, so I will now tell you stories about me. *I am God.* I do not ride this universe with a steady hand. I have often allowed you to be exactly who you wish to be without interfering or even suggesting that there is a better way. You see... I love you and I do not wish to interfere in your learning. Now we come to the problem. In learning, you are killing me. Only in that you are killing you and I am you. You are the cells and atoms of the body of God and you do not realize how important you are, and you are killing God without even knowing that you are God.

Now, I see you as unruly children who must take notice of who you really are, and so I am intervening at this time to wake you up. You have read of this in your Bibles and this time of awakening and searching for answers is called Armageddon. Only, in the Bible, you read of death and destruction and the end of the world. It is the end of the world. It is the end of a world of death and destruction and evil. The darkness is beginning to leave. Each time you choose love and kindness over anger and hatred you kill a little more darkness. The darkness is ruling the world.

The Anti-Christ, as explained in our first three books, is the altered ego, and at this time he has a strong hold in you each. He is taking over the world and he is in control at this time. The death and destruction is taking place all around you. This is it! You are at the Book of Revelations. You are fearing a dark future and you do not realize that you are in your future. Stop fearing and begin to change.

Nostradamus and many others have predicted fire and brimstone. Look around you. You have fire and brimstone now. This is not heaven on earth. This is hell. Satan is ruling this planet. Don't you see? All that you fear so much is here at hand so stop fearing it and begin to *change* it. How, you shout! Clean up you. In cleaning up you, you will clean up one entire body of darkness, and in cleaning up you – you will add one entire body to the light.

So, Armageddon is at hand and it is the battle that you now fight within you. Guilt will rise up and tell you that you are not worthy to have all that you hope and dream for. Defeat guilt. Do not listen. Do battle with fear and rise above fear to see a new age dawn. This is the Age of Aquarius and all will be battling their fears. Some will win and some will run to fight another day. Allow them their ways, as their ways are best for them. Your concern is you. You do not fight for them; you only fight your own demons. So, go get 'em!!

~❀~

You of the Universal Power of Light did not always allow ego to rule. In the beginning you were so afraid of displeasing God that you began to use ego to show you how you were right or wrong. Now you use ego to judge yourselves and to judge others. You began to use ego as a detector of wrong doing, or right doing, and he got confused and began to judge you and to judge others, and even to judge situations in your life as not good enough for you. Many times I have sent gifts to you and ego has jumped in and said, "No, this is not good enough for us. We are better than this." Now, this also works in reverse where ego says, "No, this is not right for us. We are not good enough for this gift. This is too much." And you walk on to shop some more in this big shopping center of life.

At this time you are each doing battle with ego. Ego has come to a point in his evolution where he wishes to go back to his old job of showing how God-like you are. And he is beginning to raise his head, and jump, and buck, and you are finding conflict within, and this conflict is Armageddon and you will do well in the end. You will ride your ego until you tame him and he will go back to his old job and begin to show you how you are God. So, for now you will struggle with him for a while and he will enjoy this, as he has been in control and out of place for such a long time, and he is tired and wishes to move to his right place.

So now he wants to come down from this cross that you have hung him on. In believing that you are less than God, you believe that you are not good enough to be God, and this is saying that you are undeserving and unworthy. So, it is to an extent self-punishment and I wish this punishment to end. You are God. You deserve everything that is in your creation. You belong to God and that makes you God. You deserve all that exists out there and in here. You are the creator of everyone and everything and even you. You created you and you created your neighbor, and if he has millions and you do not then you are judging you as not good enough. *There is no other reason.*

Now, some of you chose to reincarnate to learn specific lessons in this life and you believe that if you are poor it is due to this lesson you work on. So learn and stop complaining. Dig yourself out of this hole that *you* put yourself in. Take a chance. Go out on a limb. Risk until you win. You become a millionaire by taking a risk, not by playing it safe. So, teach yourself the lesson you came to learn. Go for broke. Show you how you can be everything that everyone else can be. You can be President and change the world; the entire world. The President is simply a child who *believed* he could and he did.

So, go out and take what you want from life. It is all yours. I am offering it to you daily. You receive offers and opportunities and you hold on to what you already have and do not move into a new area out of fear. Move! Change! Grow! Let you out of this trap.

You do not wish to be so out of touch with who you are, as to not know a good deal when you see one. We will all wish to grow in prosperity and this will include wealth of money, and health, and happiness, and love. You will each learn to ask for what you want and to receive what is good for you. You will make it known exactly what you want and then get out of the way and sit back and allow God to deliver.

Many of you ask for what you want and then you charge out into the world in search of it, and I will tell you that you will receive by waiting. And if you are charging around "looking for," you may miss and grab for the gold ring only to find it is brass or silver. I have the gold ring. I will deliver it to you and you will know it in time. In the beginning it may not look gold to you but trust that it is.

This is good for now as Liane wishes to communicate with me on a personal matter. Good day and please ask for help.

❧

You are all guided. You ask for help and I send help. This book is what you have asked for. You have each searched for answers and I am sending answers. This book contains information that is directed at your subconscious and even when you find it uninteresting it is most important for its content.

So now I will give you interesting information for the conscious you. You have each read our first three books and have enjoyed the secrets I shared concerning the Ten Commandments and others. This time I will tell you about marriage. *I did not ask you to wed one another.* I asked you to unite. To unite and become one is not to wed. You got confused and believed you must chain yourself to your mate and this is not what was meant. Unite means to come together, to become one. Not to force one another to change or to say vows that lock you into a future that is not what you wish. Let go of marriage.

Okay; I see I've done it again and now Liane's panicked that you'll attack, and so I will remind you for the hundredth time that *I am God.* I do not write this information to upset you, nor do I write it to amuse you. I write this information to show you who you really are. So now I am telling you to let go of marriage and I am sure that you will panic and not wish your mate to read this; "Oh no, if God does not want us to marry then he or she will leave me." Why did he or she marry you if they did not wish to? It is safe to say, "I love you and God does not care if we are married or not. He simply wants all twin souls to unite and become one. And since we *are* twins it is good to be together as long as we do not force rules and changes on one another." So, you begin to repeat this often enough and your twin will be very happy to be with you. For those of you who do not believe you are with your twin, I wish you to know that you will soon discover him or her and all will go according to plan.

Now we must deal with divorce. Get a divorce if you are not comfortable with marriage. I did not say you must remain married and I am so thankful to Liane to allow me to report this to you. She is not so sure she should allow this to channel at this time, but she is my instrument and she works for me, and she is allowing all to occur as I have requested. So, do not fear that you lose God's love in attaining a divorce. It was never my rule. I have no rules. Man, in order to control his own ego, creates the rules. He is his own worst enemy.

So now we have you divorcing and you are concerned about the children. Some of your children are much older than you. They have entered earth many times and in certain cases they were your parents, or even your husband, or wife. They are simply learning as you are learning, and the more you shelter a child the less it is allowed to grow. So, let go of this obsession to protect the innocent. You are just as naive and innocent. Let go of this desire to *use* your offspring as an excuse for doing battle. It is not good for you or for them. The offspring do not know what is going on and pick up from you, and if you deliver love to your departing spouse, the child will deliver love. *I don't care what has occurred.* A child will follow your lead. If a child is hit and his parent has taught him to be loving and forgiving he will.

A child picks up the thoughts and emotions of the parent on a telepathic level and will emit the same messages on his own level. So, now you have it. Look at your children. They are your mirrors. This is what you really think and feel. Stop denying and become open enough to look at who you are. All respond to you as you respond to yourself. If you hate you and belittle you subconsciously, you will see a child who belittles his parent and is disgusted by his parent. *Love you* and your children will love you.

Now I will discuss gays once again. I do not wish you to be so upset about this disease called AIDS. I wish you to love one another and to walk with your head high. I do not wish you to carry any more guilt than is already present in you. Your guilt is so powerful that you are creating AIDS. Go out and love all in God's creation. You do not spread AIDS any more than any other species of human. You are simply the ones who carry the greatest sexual guilt.

Now, I do suggest that you refrain from sex until you are able to *clear.* Do not believe that this is a joke. You carry this sexual guilt out of a belief that you do not deserve love. God is love and you deserve God and you deserve all that is God's. Your guilt is so powerful that it is taking over and destroying 'body.'

Once again I will remind anyone who is reading this book that if you have not read our first three books you are in your wrong place. You are not to read this book without first reading our first three books or you will cause greater fear and damage within your subconscious. This is not meant to frighten you, but *is* very important.

Now – back to my gay friends. Do not be so frightened by AIDS that you stop loving. You are beginning to cut yourselves off from God. Do not risk rejection of self in order to please those who point and blame. You are no better and you are not worse than any other. *You are God.* You chose this life style and it provides great value in the spiritual ladder to success. This lesson is simply more complicated than others. You have come to earth to learn to grow as male essence while your body is female, or, in the case of men who are gay, you have come to learn to be female essence while in male body. You do not do this out of chance. You did this out of choice. Stop punishing you for being gay. Get out into my creation and learn to be exactly who you are. You are hiding. Get out of the closet and be all that your name implies.

Gay means delight and you are delightful, and loving, and caring, and giving, and even sensual. Do not be afraid to be gay. You are killing you by your fear of you. You are not meant to be in fear. You are meant to be in love. God does not judge you and it is past time for you to stop judging you. This nonsense has gone on too long. Stop searching to find out *why* you are gay and begin searching for answers as to why you do not wish to remain gay. You are not being punished and you have every right that any other on this planet has.

You have created so much fear over your own situation that you have projected it out into my universe and now it is returning in the form of your own reflection. Look into your mirror. What you see as hatred, and anger, and revenge; it is all you – you attacking you. It is a reflection of your own desire to punish yourself for being gay.

Now, in the case of most of you who are gay we have a very big job ahead of us. I do suggest therapy. *I do not suggest any therapist who will try to convince you that you might change and go straight.* You *are* gay and you chose to be gay and this is not changeable at this time. So, get someone who believes gay to be okay! Allow him or her to conduct hypnosis on you and discover why you do not believe you deserve the fruits of life. Ask him or her to show you under hypnosis exactly where your greatest fears concerning being gay lie. Then I will begin to guide you. You will be led gently once you begin to open to self-love, however you must make the first step alone. You must wish to heal you and ask God to be with you. Ask that I guide you within and ask that I show you self-love. You must ask as I am not allowed to intervene without your permission. You are very close to submission at this time as your pain is so great. Give up and give in to God. This does not mean give up being gay. This does mean give up fighting being gay.

Now for those of you who read this and do not agree, I suggest you close this book and go about your lives without further insight into God's words to you. You are not ready for this material and I do suggest you be kind to your subconscious as well as your conscious mind and allow this information to settle in. Now I suggest you close this book.

Okay; for you who remain, we will go on to discuss further information, but this must wait until tomorrow. Liane is uncomfortable as she is blocking this and she will be well rested and ready to write for me tomorrow. When I tell you she blocks I do not mean she stops me. She simply has her own fears concerning the rest of the world and how they accept or reject her.

See; you all face your fears at this time. To you who are gay, I will tell you once again that *I am God*. And I do not judge you for being gay. I do not care if you are man, or woman, or androgynous, or even a horse. I simply want you to love who and what you are. Nothing else matters. This is why I have returned to earth. I wish you to wake up to the idea that you are me. I am you. We two are God. You and I make God. Don't hate you and don't hate your neighbor, because hate is killing God.

Once again I see it is time to begin to convince you

how *you* are God. You do not wish to believe that you are God, and you do not wish to remain *in* body, and you do not wish to remain *in* love, so we will convince you to stay. I will tell you another story.

Once upon a time in a land far away a child was born. His name was Jesus and he was king of the Jews, and he was sent to earth to guide those who could no longer find their own way back to God. You see; in these times confusion ran everyone's mind. People often became so upset with one another that they lied and called others names and told stories to make others feel or look bad. Not much has changed since this story took place has it?

So now we have this small babe and a few foretold his coming. He was seen by the psychics of his time as the Savior. They thought what they saw in their visions was a man who would save this world and create peace and love, and they eagerly spoke of his coming long before he came and they called him Savior. And now this babe has finally come and he is simply a man in a babe's form, and he wets and messes, and he did not feel like a savior. So he began to grow and he began to change and he began to have his own psychic vision, and this vision guided him. He was to lead his people out of their fear and confusion and let them know that God does care, and God is with them, and God is watching. And of course, this has been misconstrued to mean, "Look out, God watches, and he sees, and he knows, and you'll go to hell." *This is not what was meant.*

Yes I watch – as you would watch a sore or infection on your big toe. You are my big toe only you have forgotten to come back. You forget you are part of

God; part of God's body; part of the whole. You are suffering alone. You believe you are alone and fighting and struggling to survive and you are not alone. I'm here. I'm looking down at my big toe and I see your pain and I see how to heal you, and you are so busy washing out the infection that you are panicked and you do not realize that the infection itself must stop. You continue to wash away the pus when you could stop this pus. *Stop hating you.* You create mountains of new pus by hating you. It is not the infection *it is the cause* you must look at.

So now we have God's big toe infected and this hurts. God hurts. He has no control over what the cells are doing. *He can only hold his foot up* to stop the throbbing as blood pumps into his toe. He cannot stop this infection. The cells of the body must do the work they were trained to do. Cells reproduce 'like' cells, and heal and rebuild. Only now you see the problem. *You produce 'like,'* and 'like' for you at this time is fear, and you are reproducing fear in place of love.

So, I have decided to step in, to intervene; to stop this infection only by aid. I am sending aid. A Band-Aid (bandage) if you will, to cover this infection until it is allowed to drain; to clear up sufficiently to warrant fresh air and new scar tissue to form. I am giving you time to heal and I am holding you up in this universe as you heal. Do you get the idea?

Now we see how your Bible becomes so confusing. God says we are no better than a big toe and we are infected with pus and he will raise us up. Put this one down on paper and see what you do with it in the year 4001.

You'll be shocked at its meaning by that time and no one will be living by the rules you have written for them any more than they do now.

So, back to this Christ child who has come to save the world. He came to show you how you are God, to clear the cobwebs of your subconscious mind, to allow you to remember that you have a job to do. Your job is love. Love you and love everyone. "Big job," you say. You bet it is, and I for one find it difficult at times to express my love for those who are cutting me out of their lives. You have projected all thoughts back to the body, and the body who holds you up is having trouble, because you send an imbalance of negative thought which is energy.

So, now you are beginning to affect the source by your energy. Energy is God thought. God thought is projected by all who think and these thoughts affect the source and to offset this imbalance it is necessary to send love. Thoughts of love and kindness will save all in this hemisphere and beyond to others. You are not alone. I hold you up as others rush around seeking medicine to heal the infection.

Some have decided to evacuate earth and they channel to those on earth who will listen and they tell them how they are prepared to assist. And now you have many believing that aliens who love you will take you off this planet until the pain goes away. Do not run. Do not leave earth. You are copping out; finding a hiding place. We need each and every cell to heal and rejuvenate. We will *all* heal and if you choose to leave, you will be returned to earth after this healing process and you will not fit in. You will have missed salvation. You will have missed the graduation ceremony.

Don't run. Become love and light. If you choose to rise off this planet you will be infection leaving the main sore, and when you return you will be infection returning to a healed wound and you will re-infect the good work that is being done. Don't go away and hide. Stay with us. We will save you from yourself and you may then save me from your thoughts.

I do not wish to go into further detail at this time, as further information will short circuit my pen and she is valuable to me. The information I give is received by her and creates great changes in her subconscious to the point that she becomes weak and does not enjoy the full energy she loves. So I will be kind and give her smaller doses for now. She wishes to enjoy writing for God and I wish to make it a joyful experience for her. She will be recharged again soon and she will be happy to write again.

Now I will tell you another story. Once upon a time all went well and everyone loved and danced and sang out in joy, and the time is now. Love you and you become the savior. It is so simple. Allow you to be exactly who you are and you will be unconditional love. If your job is to kill for a living get out of your job and continue to love yourself; and do not judge yourself for killing, and I do not judge you for killing. You are simply learning how to overcome death.

So for now I leave you to contemplate on who Christ is. He is not me and he is not you. He is unconditional love who projected into a fetus and he came to show you your way, and he lost his way at times. This darkness that permeates from earth is powerful and only love is more powerful. Do not spread the word of God by force or fear tactics. This is not love.

ﷺ

You do not believe that you are God and that you deserve to receive as God. You are so afraid to *be* God that you do not allow others their right to be God. You get so upset if one of you claims to be God. One of you will always claim to be God, as I am you, and you do not wish to acknowledge me as your source. Stop separating yourself from God. You claim to be human, and you claim to feel love, and I tell you now that this love is me. I am love; this force that drives you to constantly search for another, or even an animal to love.

So many of you are beginning to replace human love with animal love. You buy a dog, or cat, or bird, and begin to love it, and cherish it, only because it is easy for you. Animals love unconditionally. If you accidentally step on your pet, he forgives you within minutes. If you punish your pet, he will not hate you, and he will forget his punishment the moment you hug him again. Love heals quickly in the animal kingdom. This is due to the strong instinctual pattern that remains for animals.

You have lost your instincts. You became so

confused about what was best that you gave up on your own good sense of what is best. You allow others to train you by giving them power to say, "Yes, this is good for you," or, "No you won't do well with this." Let go of this desire to allow others to show you who you are. They can only show you who they are. They are not you and they do not exist in your form, and believe me when I say that they will not pay the price for what they have suggested for you. You pay your own price. You reap what you sow. They do not. They tell you how to live and when the going gets tough they are quickly gone. So, I wish you to use your animal instinct and you will be doing what is best for you, not what is best for them and whatever lesson they are working on.

So – back to our animal lovers. Those of you who have replaced human love with animal love will wish to know that this is a good place to learn, and then begin to apply what you learn to humans. Be as loving and kind to humans as you are to your pet. Allow all to flow. If you wish to pick up your pet and hug him, you do. If he fights to get away you giggle and say, "Oh no you don't – I love you and I want a hug." This is how I wish you to show unconditional love to humans. Tell them you love them and you insist on a hug.

Hugs are very good for you. When you hug you generate high levels of energy that circle between your auric fields and mix your energy with the field of the one you hug. Hugging is therapy. Hug and hug and hug. Hug a stranger if you get the urge. So often you feel this urge to reach out and hug; only you stop yourself out of belief that you will look silly or be refused. You will not be refused. No one can refuse a hug. It is like refusing God. You cannot refuse the essence of who you are and who you are is God.

Now, for those who do not believe in God I wish to explain how you too are God. You are love. Believe in love and the value of love and you believe in God. Believe in thought power and you believe in God. Believe in energy and you believe in God. Believe in you and you believe in God.

You cannot 'not' be God. God is simply a word – a descriptive word to show who *you* are. Change my name and you change nothing. I am still the source; the power unit; the energy; the original thought; the original energy that began to move, and expand, and grow, and send out from the source to the outskirts of creation and back again, to recharge and send out again in a pattern of eternal reaction and combustion, to grow and expand beyond myself and on into life everlasting, and I do not require a title. If you do not believe in God you will believe in whatever you wish. You will create something to believe in, as you must. To believe in goodness or kindness is to believe in God. God is simply a name and names are easily changed.

Norman is Liane's choice for me at times. See how this name takes away all your fears concerning who I am. If I were to write these books to you and call myself Norman, you would express a different view of all that you have read here. Now we have this odd guy by the name of Norman spouting off about love and such, and this guy is a little off beat, but we think we like him. So now you take away my holiness and I am just one of you expressing thoughts, and you see how I express, and you even begin to accept me as somewhat of a genius, and you may wish to get to know me better.

Now, give me back the name God and everyone stands back and holds back opinions on what I write, and believes that this all hinges on whether or not you accept this as the true word of God. And if you decide no, then you will run away and not listen to any of this. And if you decide yes, you will begin to push this information at others in hopes that they agree with your findings. And I will tell you now that you do not do well to push your beliefs on another.

You are killing one another over your beliefs. You are not doing well with this loving business. Let go of this desire to change someone else into you. You want everyone to be as *you* think they should be. You want your lover to dress the way you want him to, and you want your parents to act the way you think is best, and your way is simply that... *your* way. So allow him to be a slob if he dresses so, and allow your mother to nag and worry if she wishes to, and you will be allowing yourself to be who you are simply by allowing others to be who they are. This is the easiest way to love you. Let others be, and in letting them be you are letting you be.

We are all here to learn. I send you your mirror so you may see who you are. If you see a nagging mother in your mirror it is your reflection of how you treat you. If you see a hateful father, you are seeing your inner hate for self. If you see a father who has run away from his responsibility, it is you running away from who you are. You do not wish to be you. You are not good enough, not smart enough, or pretty enough, or fun and exciting to be with, so you desert and you run. And I send a father to you who is willing to be your mirror and run away to show you who you are.

Now I wish to address child molestation. If you have been molested as a child I wish you to know that you did not deserve to be with this person. In your mind you did not deserve love and your mirror showed you the pain of physical sex without attachment of love. You were molested to show yourself how little you love you. You were taught through this experience how to love another sexually without loving spiritually, and you will find that in your current relationship, you do not love from spirit. You may feel this as love but you will not experience real love until you leave this lesson behind and learn to love you. How do you leave this lesson? You say, "I am sorry I did not love me, and I am sorry that I judged those who molested me."

You may wish to go under hypnosis as Liane has. She was molested and did not know. She was guided to hypnosis as she did not believe when I told her. And under hypnosis she was allowed to see and hear and re-experience. I do suggest recording your session, as you will often doubt what you know to be true. And this recording will allow you to convince your conscious mind that these situations do indeed exist for you.

I will now tell you a good story. You who are

molesters will enjoy this one. I am God and I sit in judgment of no man, woman, or child. You each learn and grow and I will allow you to do what you choose in order to grow. Know that you are overriding the will of another when you take a child who is not prepared psychologically to fight you off. That will do for now. Do not judge this information. Judgment creates judgment and what you send out you get back.

≈

I now wish to discuss gays and their right to "be." You all believe yourselves to be different and odd and out of alignment. I am asking that you see yourselves as normal. You are normal in that you are not abnormal. You have been taught that what you do is abnormal and I will tell you once again how you as spirits entered form. You entered to experience love, and emotion, and sense, and vibrate, and hear, and see. Only through form might you feel and experience.

So now you have zapped into this fetus, and you are small, and you are punished, or screamed at, whenever you touch you. This is the silliest of man's rules. Do not play with you. Do not touch and experiment and feel how you are. We are taught on earth that to touch our sex organs is embarrassing to others. And so we begin to judge ourselves as doing wrong, and here we have it... sexual guilt begins in the crib. You don't stand a chance. You begin to believe it is wrong to touch your anus, or your penis, or your vagina, and now we have you all so guilty about sex that you cannot even speak these titles for your own body parts. Your guilt of being sexual is so great that you find it vulgar to mention your own body by name. You call them your private parts, and you teach your children to hide them, and to hold on to any guilt that you are holding on to. And in holding on to this guilt, you are killing all you teach in such a fashion.

Do not get on your high horse and run from this information. I am here to help you and I cannot help you if you do not listen. If you close your mind simply because you are embarrassed we will not make it. This is important. Stop judging this information and stop judging me. I am God and I see no problem with your body, or touching your body, or looking at your body, or loving your body. You are neglecting you. You refuse to touch or even look at you and now your body is dying.

You were never meant to die. You hate being in body and you judge body as ugly, and you judge your personal parts as vulgar, and you are killing you by judging you. Your bodies are shutting down out of lack of love. Your relationships are falling apart because you do not love who you are. You do not enjoy good sex because your guilt gets in the way, and so you force yourself to make love even though you don't "feel" like it. Or you give the excuse of a headache, or stress, or you are tired. Sex is love, love expressed as sex. Love, love, love. Get this straight. *I do not judge you. You* made all these silly rules concerning sex, and love, and marriage, and who, and when, and even how. You do not do well with rules and I suggest you get rid of them.

Now, I wish to discuss gays and their right to be gay and their right to make love in whatever fashion they choose. *No one on earth has the right to tell another how to live.* Now, if you think you are morally fit and that I do not speak as God, I wish you to go within in meditation and prayer and ask me to show you who I am, and it will be done. Do not mistake this as a threat or a joke. I am tired of all this nonsense. You are acting as though God does not care that you are making pain for yourselves and I do care. In every possible aspect, I care. You are not the only civilization to which I have communicated and you will not be the last. No one believes God speaks to his people and it's time you began to listen.

Now, go to your mirror and look at, and touch *all* of you. Learn to love your body, for only in loving you can you love others, as you are all there is. You are all "one." When you judge them as vulgar, it comes right back at you. When you let them be, it comes right back at you. When you love and accept them, you are loving and accepting you. Now, I do hope I have not frightened you with this information. I value our students and I believe it is time to go deeper into the causes of your guilt and fears. In looking at who you are, you will begin to see who you really are. Good day to you all.

You do not believe that you are the source of all that comes to you. You believe that you are coming into your own good out of luck, or frequent accident, or even failure to be out of the way when something good occurs. You tell your friends how you were just lucky, or in the right place at the right time, and I will tell you that there is no right place or right time. There only *is*.

The right time is always now and the only reason you do not receive now is your desire to be left out. This desire comes from self-inflicted punishment. For one reason or another you do not believe that you deserve, and so you continue to neglect yourself. And when I send someone to love and cherish you, you send them away and say he or she is not right for you, or he or she does not push your buttons.

And now we see you rejecting a gift without trying it out, and once you have spent some time with this person, they just may be someone special to you. How often have you heard someone say how they were not interested in their mate in the beginning, but grew to love him or her in time? The reason you are not interested in the beginning, is because this person has come to show you something about you that you do not wish to see. So now we have you wondering how many, and how often you should fall in love, and I say every time you see someone. I want you to begin to fall in love with everyone who comes to you, until you no longer hold judgments as to who is right or wrong for you.

All are right in that I will continue to send them for you to learn. And once you learn, you may go on to others, and still others after them. This will eventually teach you to stop judging who they are, and how they look, and how they speak, and how they live. And before you know it, you will stop judging *you* for how you live, and how you speak, and how you dress, and how you act.

So, my gift to you at this time are the mirrors in your life. Stop turning your back on your mirror. We will not learn to overcome judging others by running from them. Judgment is not light. All light is God. Judgment is fear based, in that it is darkness, and it began "the fall" in the first place. You began to judge others as better than yourself, and you began to learn to compete, and you are still judging and competing, and you are still falling.

Now, for those who are now with your twin and do not wish to wander, you will see yourselves in others. These will be friends and relatives, and I do expect you to take a good look at who you are, and do not judge them. Now, go in peace and know that I love you.

You do not wish to be with the ones that I send to you to show you who you are. You look at these people and find them undesirable and you send them on their way or you simply run and hide from them. I wish you to begin to go into your fears. Be with those who make you uncomfortable until you *are* comfortable. They are simply you. They are your mirror. They reflect who you are. If you find them loud and obnoxious, it is your own self-hate of how you see you on a subconscious level. If you see them as friendly and unloving, it is you being your own friend but holding back your own personal love. If you see them as pragmatic it is your own pragmatism. If you see them as foreigners it is your own fear of you not fitting in, and if you see them as less than you it is your own attitude that you are less than.

Now, I wish to take this time to address race. To be part of a minority race is not inferior in any way, shape, or form and I will not wish you to believe such foolishness. You are different because you chose to be a minority and you do not fit-in in this country because you were taught that you do not deserve to "be." Allow all past discretion to die. Let go of who you are and who your ancestors are and begin to blend. Stop fighting to be special and begin to accept your special self as you are. You are fighting for what you already have. You are special. You are even different than most, so stop fighting for recognition. *You have recognition*; more than you know what to do with.

Now, I wish you to begin to love. Love the white man and love the yellow man and red man and black man and all who are different than yourselves. In loving others you will be loving God and in loving God you will love you. Stop wallowing in self-defiance and begin to rise up and *love*. You have hated and feared being different for so long that you do not know who you want to be anymore. You have begun to change your looks to fit in when what you need to change is your attitude. You have been raised in fear and you have been taught to not trust. And when you begin to let go of un-trusting and un-loving, you will begin to rise up. You are buried deep within your fears. Love will raise you up to light. You have been taught to be less than who you are and when you begin to accept who you are, you will begin to be accepted.

You chose to be different. It is not by accident. It is not a punishment; it *is* your own choice. You decided to learn to overcome fear at a time when fear was predominant, and this fear is now taking over in the world. Stop living in fear. *Love!* You have been oppressed to the extent that you do not know how to change who you are, and I will tell you now that *there are no victims.*

So now you sit and judge me as being harsh and uncaring and I am harsh on this subject and I do care. I care enough to say how *you* can change your entire world. You can rise up and rule, or lead, or march with the best. You too may have it all. You too are the children of God. You too will come home to me and you too will be with me in this Second Coming. Being part of a minority is a big lesson just as being gay is. Do not be so concerned with your current situation, as you are all children of God and you chose to be in a situation that is most difficult to overcome in order to learn to "overcome." So get on with the work you came to do.

You too may become all that you desire by simply learning to love yourself "as you are" and changing what you do not love in regards to your current situation. Stop bemoaning your lot in life and begin to act as though you are God. Simply be God and your suffering will end and your mind will change as to how you are being treated or not respected or in many cases simply not accepted. *Acceptance brings acceptance.* This is most important for you to know at this time... accept... accept... accept. You can change everything you see by loving unconditionally, just as everyone else has to do.

This is all for now as I wish you to think on what I have said for some time. I will return tomorrow with more good news for my students. All of you are me. Each and every one of you is God becoming God. Do not be so sure that you were always black or always white or yellow or red. We change often, and if you chose black this time, you may return again as white to reap what you have sown, so don't be so quick to hate any other colors.

And now for you who think you are better than any other color. You too will have the opportunity to return and experience as the color you hate and you too will reap your own harvest. It is law. What goes out comes right back to you. So, now we have it. God has finally made a law, only I did not make it, you did. This is another of your many rules, and you chose this one to keep you from getting too carried away with who you are and how you live. And this one has caused a great deal of pain. If you will simply let go of this belief, you will see that you may learn without re-experiencing again. This is truth. You may choose to learn out of love instead of punishment. You now fear what may happen if you do not love, so you love.

I will tell you now that what you believe is what you get. If you believe you do not need re-affirmation on this subject of reincarnating to learn both sides of this coin, you may walk away and simply know without experiencing. This will upset many who teach strongly that what goes around comes around, but you will get over it. I have decided to tell you how it really is and this is it. You do not have to reincarnate to learn. You may simply watch and learn, or you may select portions of a lesson to work on, or you may forego lessons altogether. It is not necessary to come to earth to learn to be God. You have become so confused that you believe you must continue to return until you get it right. You already are God. Let me explain. You came to earth as God to play and experiment. You were having a good ol' time until you created opposing forces. "The fall." Competition. Believing in fear. One less than another.

So now we have God stuck in matter and he wants out. He wants to go back to the God force; the source – me; I say, "Okay, you got stuck, you get unstuck." You say, "Oh no, this is my lesson and I must do this till I get out." I say, "Okay, if that's what you wish." You say, "It must be what is best." I say, "If you believe it, then it is." You say, "Oh shit." And here we have you millenniums later and still stuck and still believing you must learn to be God, when you cannot learn to be what you already are, and so I have come through one of you to say so now. You may believe me and come home whenever you are ready or you may stay and struggle with lessons. The choice is yours and it always has been.

Now, how do we get home? We ascend. One at a time at first, then in groups, then in larger groups, then in great groups, then as civilizations, and we all go back to God. And how do we ascend? We change from matter to energy – and how? We raise our vibration and this as we know from our first three books is done by clearing our own bodies to allow them to vibrate at a much higher rate. And this allows them to rise up, and this allows them to walk into the light of God once again.

So, *clean out you* and get out of this mess you have created. You will not rise up by moaning and sobbing and carrying on about the injustices there. Get out of your own way and see how simple this is. Get out of my way and let me in. Get out of your way and allow yourself love. Get out of my way and allow me to guide you home. Get out of this big circle of confusion. Earth was meant to be a playground and you have turned it into a pharmaceutical test tube. Get out. Leave all this by cleaning it up.

You *can* change you and in changing you, you change destiny, and laws of the universe, and any other restrictions you are placing on yourselves and others. You are not meant to be here... not like this. This was fun... not hell. Get out. Pack your bags and take responsibility for your own personal mess, and we will rise up and ascend.

God does not wish to be left out of any part of you. You do not wish to allow me in to many parts of your life. I have been shut out and shut up for years and now I want the opportunity to speak. In the beginning I did not care to communicate with you as you did not wish help. You believed yourselves to be in good condition and you believed me to be the one who put you there. Now you believe yourselves to be in hell and you scream to be let out and you are screaming so loud that I can no longer ignore you.

So, here I am and I might add that I don't seem to be receiving the attention that is due me. I wish to be received with love, and acceptance, and appreciation, and instead I am received with judgments, and speculation, and even jeering. "No, this can't be God. He's not like this." Or, "No, this isn't him, he wouldn't use these words." Or even, "No, he doesn't discuss such subjects. As we all know, God is holy, and a supreme being, and he does not talk like we talk, and he would not tell us not to look at our bodies with distaste, and how we all hate being in form. And God just does not do these things. But we find this all very interesting, and maybe this girl is channeling something from inside of her, or maybe she is channeling someone who will eventually trick us, or maybe she channels evil, or maybe she is haywire and she does not pick up the correct signals."

And I sit here as you read and re-read portions of these books, and I wonder how long it will take to get through to you. And I think this will take some time so I will continue to write, and Liane will continue to allow me to write, and one day even she will "know" that I am God. You see... she too has her doubts. She too does not wish to be tricked. She too fears being made to look foolish for writing for God, if he should turn out to be explained as some strange part of her that is simply connected, in some way, to the universe. And what would become of her and her beliefs if all this were simply a trick.

So, here you have it. I do not expect anyone to believe that I am indeed God. You do not have the ability at this time to see me as I am. I am not who you believe me to be, and in telling you how I am I would upset you even more. So, for now, I will continue to write for you. And Liane will continue this work, as she has grown to love me and she does not care who or what I am, so much as she cares about helping you up, out of your pain.

Now, God is in every living and non-living entity on this planet. God does not restrict himself to human form and God does not write this for you out of disgust, or anger, or hate, or even revenge. God is writing to you out of love. God does not wish to create more confusion for you and the best way to keep you free of confusion is to give you small doses of important information, in order to open your subconscious. And once we open the door we will gradually take a look at what is stored there. And once you look at your attic, you will be seeing how you are manipulated and directed into the events that shape you. And once you see how you are manipulated you will see how to change. And once you change you will become better, and then best, and then rise up out of this mess.

This mess that you see on earth is simply a reflection of this mess within. *Clean up your mess!* Go within to your subconscious and look at who you are, and begin to take responsibility for your own mistakes. These are not sins. No one ever sins. If you see you as a barbarian, it is simply you being God. If you see you as a minister who dies defending his church, it is simply you being God, and if you see you having an affair with other than a spouse it is simply you being God. God does not work in God's own light. God has moved out of his light and into darkness and this was never meant to be, and now I wish to return to the light.

I do not condemn you nor do I judge you for your actions. You are simply me being you, and you do not know that you are me. You celebrate this custom of dressing in costume for your celebration at certain times, and this is where you are now. You dressed up as someone, or something else, and you went out to a party and you forgot to come home and remove your costume. And now you have worn this costume for so long, that you walk around and "act" like the character you have dressed as. You are not that person. You are simply in costume. You are not a witch, or a ghoul, or a monster, or a prince, or princess, or maid, or mayor, or king, or beggar, or even the milk maid you play. You are God.

You got so wrapped up in being in costume that you began to believe that this is you and this is not you. This is the outside of what you have projected into, and can be changed into whatever you desire. You are not who you believe. You got stuck in your costume; and out of fear you stayed stuck, and now you walk around believing you "are" the costume. *You are not human.* You are God. You have begun to believe that you are human and I will tell you now that you are not. You walk around and act out this role and it is time to quit. *You are God.* You got stuck. You believe you are Donald Duck, or Mickey Mouse, or even a giant pumpkin. Whatever costume you donned once long ago for fun, you now wear on a daily basis and you forgot that you are wearing it.

So now we must get you out of this costume so that I may show you who you really are, and you want to hold on to this costume for dear life, as you believe this costume *is* you, and you do not wish to lose you. *Lose you!* It is best. Let go of who and what you are. Walk out into the sunshine, and know that you have been stripped and you have nothing left to hold on to, and you will be letting go of who you are. You are not the costume. You are not human. You are not businessman, or show producer, or waitress, or carpenter, or car salesman. You are so much more and I want you to give up this silly game and stop pretending to be what you are not.

You may begin to peel off your costume one piece at a time. Go within. Go into your subconscious and see who you really are. You are not God. You are light and love, and you will become God by allowing light and love to channel through you to others. You may change this world by changing you, and you may change you by going into your subconscious.

So now we must find the door to the subconscious and this is easily achieved. Within eight months after my pen began to enema she began to "see" who she was in past life. In seeing past life she began to "realize" that she was much more than simply her job in this life. In realizing how much more she was, she began to "see" how she does not live on earth, but only returns here for lives. And in seeing that earth is not her only home, she began to realize that she did not live in body alone, and in "realizing" this she now knows that she is more than body, and less than whole, and she is now working on becoming whole.

She does enema daily and brings other parts of her, living in other dimensions, into focus and releases their subconscious debris through this body. She has only one physical form and has released the past lives of others, who are her, through this form. And as she clears these lives she communicates with these others, who were once her, and she knows how time does not exist so these others, who are her, are living now just as she is. And she has allowed all of her past lives to channel through this form in order to release subconscious debris from many lives. And she does not now, nor will she, understand how this is done.

You too will come to a place in enema where you will have *connected* with your subconscious and past lives, and you too will begin to "see" who you really are. Do not give up on you. You are the key to this universe and beyond. You have no idea how vast you are and how many you affect. You eat an apple and you feed millions. You put drugs into your body and you drug millions. You clean out this body and you clean out millions. You are the answer to this universe and you do not even know the question.

The question is this. If you *are* God, how did you

get here? Why did you come? How long have you been in this state and when will you leave? "Not such simple answers," you say. Yes. I believe you are correct.

So I will now begin to tell you how long, and why, and from where, and when. You will do well to look at who you are, and in seeing you, you will see God. God does not wish to be left out any longer. Let me into the body. I wish to reign and to save the light. Go now and know that you are so much more than a costume. You are the light of this galaxy and you are growing dim. I will recharge you. You need only ask. Ask for God's light to shine through you and you will receive me.

⚛

*S*o now I have you all wondering how it is that I have come to you at this time. After all, God does not sit down and write to you often – not that you consciously are aware of. So, I will tell you. You are at the beginning of a great new adventure and you are about to see how this universe *is*. You will wish to know that I do not wish to be with you in death and destruction, so you are now being moved to peace and love.

You are not to be so quick to judge others as the bad guys. *There are no bad guys.* So, here we have a dilemma. How can I be God, and say that wrong does not exist? I will tell you now that I do not agree with killing, and I do not agree with death and destruction, and I do not agree with punishing the self with guilt and illness. And I will tell you too that I do not agree with capital punishment, and I do not agree with sexual harassment, and I do not agree with pain; and harmony must reign once again on this planet.

STOP FIGHTING. Stop punishing one another and stop killing one another and learn to live and let be. Stop trying to control the thoughts and actions of another, and stop standing in the way of peace and harmony for all. *You* are hampering the Second Coming by not being in your right place. Your right place is to love all unconditionally and to accept all who come to you and to stop judging one as better than or less than another.

You are the only one in God's way because you are all there is. If you will just wake up and get out of your own way, we will have peace on earth and good will toward man. It is not so difficult as you believe. I speak to you now, and you read and you know that it *is* me and you do not attempt to remove the blockages from your body that will allow you to rise up and see. How can you not want to be one of the first to say yes to God? And why aren't you doing your work for God? Maybe you forgot to clear today and God can't get in. Here we go again. I begin to mention enema and you scream and shout that there must be an easier way. Why in heavens name are you so afraid to rinse out your tubing? What's the big deal?

You put chemicals and waste and toxins and drugs into these same tubes on a daily basis, and now someone like God suggests enema and you freak out. You begin to call it dangerous and explain the pitfalls and I, for one, am beginning to believe you have really gone too far in this worship of fear and fear tactics. Give me a break by giving you a break. Enema will not kill you, it will clear you. It will not end your life; it will begin your life. It will not injure you, it will heal you. Get down off your soapbox and give it a try.

So, now I have exhausted Liane once again. She is in pain as I channel this information to you, as she "feels" responsible to you for what I write, and she does not wish to write about something that is believed to be disgusting by most. So God will move on to less painful topics and allow her body to rest. You see, she does not write these books... *I do*. And when I discuss enema she begins to tense, and her fear of rejection rises, and I must fight my way through to allow you to read this information.

We could avoid this pain to Liane... I could simply write what is convenient to her, meaning I could stick to the subjects she agrees with and wishes to share with you. How would you like that? A censored God once again. No; that's not what you have asked for. You, who read this material, have asked for "the real McCoy," and now you have him and you're not so sure you want him to be this real. Too bad. You get just what you ask for on earth. And enough of you have had enough of forgery and fakeness; and in your quest for truth you have asked to be awakened and I am now channeling into this dimension to *wake you up*.

Here you have it. God has come to earth to help and you don't approve of God's game plan, so you move right along with your life, just as though I didn't speak with you. What will it take to wake you up? Do you want tricks and signs from heaven? And how many signs and how often must I create miracles? I have created miracles on this planet for centuries and still you do not have faith. I walk this planet at times and speak with my children, and someone comes along and says, "Don't tell anyone you talk with God daily or you will be locked up," and so you see my problem.

I do speak with many of you. Why can't you all simply accept one another? Why must one of you be uncomfortable because you do not fit the mold of another? This is not Godliness. You are each special and each God. Get yourselves together and begin to love and accept. Do not ridicule those who are different, as you too may soon be different. Let them believe in God. Let them believe in angels and let them believe in miracles.

You want miracles now and I tell you, you have one. This book is written for God and by God thanks to the use of someone's body. I only needed a foothold to begin my work; someone who was not afraid when God spoke up and said, "I want to talk to you." And now I have my foothold and had she kept it all to herself you would not see this book in print.

You too will have choices to make when you decide to work for God. I wish you well with your choices and I wish you well with your "coming out" into God's army. The more of you who let go of your fear and shout out what you are doing, the faster we will all catch on. Don't hide when you could dance, and sing, and laugh with joy that we are on our way to ascension. We are not alone. There are many who have worked quietly for years and now it is time to stand up and be counted.

❧

Once upon a time I did not wish to be man. I tried to block what I could and I tried to not look at who I was. Now I am God and I do not wish to be hidden in man. Man is you and you are beginning to see me as part of you. Now I wish you to see me as all of you. You do not separate God parts and man parts. Man is God. God is man. I am you in every way. I am your brain, I am your liver, I am your fallopian tubes, I am your inner organs, I am your skin, I am your nails, I am your hair, I am your sex organs, I am your eyes, and I am your tongue. I do not stop being man anywhere in you. I am *all* of you. You do not exist where I do not exist. I am the part of you that thinks, and the part of you that judges, and the part of you that forgives, and the part of you that is love. I do not at any point stop being you. You cannot separate me from you. If you hate part of you, you hate me. If you hate your hands, if your feet are too big, if you dislike your hair, it is all me. You are criticizing God and I do not wish to be criticized.

Now, I do not expect you to love and hug your feet and hands and hair. I do, however, expect you to love and hug you. Hug your own body. Hug other bodies as well.

Hugging is healing and healing makes God. You will all wish to be God and hugging is a good place to start. I wish you to learn to touch one another. In touching, you are generating interest in sex. I wish you to touch and generate love. You began to believe that to touch one another is to begin sex and this is not as it should be. To touch is to love. To hug is to share and to see through eyes of love is best.

So, I wish to give you a homework assignment. Hug at least three times each day until you are well. You will know when you are well because you will ascend. You will begin to vibrate so rapidly that you will rise up and you will go back to God. God is not the only one who is not in his right place. You too remain in your wrong place. Soon we will straighten this mess out and you will rise up and join me and know that you are God. When you know that you are God, you will begin to act like God. You will love all who walk this planet and you will love all who come to your door.

Do not fear those who judge you as crazy and do not fear those who call you liar at this time. You do not know who I am and you do not know that you are me. Soon you will know, and to be called names for your beliefs will not be so painful. I encourage you to step forward and say who you are, and in doing so, you allow others to say who they are. You need not fight or argue. Just state simply how you see me and how you see you, and this will allow others to know that they too may come forward, and soon you will see how big my army truly is. You will not wish to hide when you begin to love each and everyone who comes to you regardless of their claims. You will be so sure of who you are that who they are will be clear also. For now I wish you love, as love brings love, and I wish you joy, as joy brings joy, and I wish you hugs, as hugs allow you to vibrate and will bring you God.

I will now teach you a new lesson. This one is on drugs. You are all drug addicts, as no one is 'not' addicted to drugs. Some take drugs for fun. Some take drugs to sleep. Some take drugs to live. Some take drugs to allow a part of them to be pain free. Others take drugs daily on their own in the form of nicotine or caffeine. If you take either of these you are addicted. I don't care if it's once a month. These drugs are addictive and when you return to them it is out of a pleasant feeling, and this pleasant feeling is the addiction. If you do not "realize" you have this pleasant feeling it does not change this addiction. You would not put it in your mouth if it did not once "feel" good.

So, now you drink caffeine in sodas, and coffee, and tea, and you smoke cigarettes, and chew tobacco, and I will wish this to end. No more numbing the senses to feel less pressure. *No more drugs.* Please stop the intake of drugs. You are killing the cells of your body. You fight for fair treatment of others and yet you poison you daily. You are so confused on this subject. You are literally allowing this body to die without concern for its welfare. Why? Because someone said it was okay to do just a little damage; one or two hits off marijuana is okay; one cigarette won't kill you; a drink now and then calms the nerves. You are so confused that you put tons of chemicals into your bodies in a single year. If I were to empty your bodies of debris and show you how much toxic waste you contain, you would move out of the neighborhood in fear of this new chemical dump site.

This is enough. Stop this incessant need for chemicals. Those preservatives are not good for you and are breaking you down. They do not add to you, they draw from you. They are chemicals. Don't you see? Chemicals — that stuff that kills just by breathing its toxic air. Chemicals, in tiny doses in your food for all your life. Figure it out. It's not safe. You are not safe. Go to the store and read the labels. Look at what you have put into your body on a daily basis and multiply that by weeks, and months, and years, and you will see what you are. You are turning into chemical and are no longer natural. The soul cannot function in a house that is not made of God. God is natural he is not chemical.

Now, I don't want you to freak out and begin to push others to clean out and clean up. This is *your* project. You are others, and in cleaning you out the others will follow. No pushing. No bribery. Just show them how good it can be.

There are a great number of healthy foods at good prices in your health food store. Find a large store with a big variety. Stop eating chemicals and preservatives and you will stop aging. Chemicals break down the chromosomes and create havoc within the blood stream, and the blood stream nurtures the entire body. Do not smoke as it is hard on your lungs. Do not smoke cigarettes as they are very bad for you and you see their effect at all times. So many of you are killing yourselves that you simply look the other way when someone lights up. Don't look the other way. Get up and move away. This is not rude... this is saving you. You will intake the smoke filled air and now you too are killing God one cell at a time.

So, no more chemicals. No more alcohol, and no more use of preservatives and chemicals. Sugar is not a chemical, however, sugar reacts within the body as a drug and is best to avoid. I want you all operating at maximum potential when we rise up. So, go to your health food stores and buy fresh muffins, and breads, and fruits, and vegetables, and natural chips, and peanut butter, and jams, and jellies. Yes; they have it all in all the correct forms. Be sure to read labels as some health food establishments are also delis and this creates confusion. I love you and I wish you well in your search for perfection.

This is how we get back to God. A perfect God is a holy God, and a holy God is an ascending God. You will begin to vibrate at a rapid speed and rise up off this planet, and to vibrate we must clear and clean out our carburetor, and pump good clean powerful gas through our system. So for now I suggest that you do as you wish and soon you will be guided to change. You will not rush to your refrigerator and toss everything into the garbage. This will be a gradual process. I will allow you to cheat for a short time, and soon you will begin to feel me nudge you to change what you eat, and to drop your addictions, and you will feel quite comfortable in the process of change. For now I wish you to "know" this information so you may make your own decisions and choices based on knowledge, and we all will be better for it.

Now I wish to discuss purity – purity of soul. Your soul is pure and will remain so. It does not wish to return to form until the form is pure also. This may take a little time but the process is beginning. Souls are beginning to see a light where they might re-enter form. Once in form, they will be allowed to do their work and to follow the master game plan. So, let's encourage our soul to re-enter body by cleaning our body up a bit. We wash our face and brush our teeth, but that is like washing the outside of a food container that is no longer in use. The food is gone and its debris is hard and dry inside this container, and the owner washes up the outside and does not flush the inside. Let's get going on this clean-up business.

Okay; I see that I am boring you once again with all this talk of changing you and cleaning you out, so I'll get to the good stuff. You are so sure that you have all the answers that I might as well leave you to your own destruction. How would that be? Create your messes and figure out what you've done yourselves. I'll just sit up here and watch. You do it your way and I'll sit here in all my holiness and wait for you to catch on. Of course that may take a few million years and by then body will have extinguished itself, and you will have a new form that is primarily debris and is unable to vibrate, and without vibration it will not function properly.

So you will have deformed humans who actually are missing parts, as with those who are created after Agent Orange, and other chemicals have been breathed and ingested into the body. *The body is not meant to take in chemicals in any amount, no matter how small or large, and the effects will eventually be the same. Chemically deformed babies are your mirror. Look closely at this mirror, as you are now creating future generations of deformity by your constant intake of chemicals, drugs, preservatives and even sugar. You have gone haywire and you do not realize that you have lost your grip on who your are, and how to eat and breathe properly.*

I wish you to begin to live naturally and to eat naturally. This will become important to you at some point and I will guide you into this change with the least amount of pain for you. Some will become ill and be forced to quit bad habits and others will walk into this change easily. For those who become ill, I wish you to know that this is your choice. You do not wish a gradual process as you wish to teach yourself the power of your own will and spirit. Do not suggest to others that they are crippling themselves as this will turn them away. We work on ourselves in this class.

My favorite song is Mr. Jackson's "Man in the Mirror." I inspired this song and I still enjoy it. I wish you all to eat good healthy foods and enjoy life. I am not so sure you will like to become a robot, but if you continue as you are, that is what you are becoming. The debris in your body controls your actions. You punish yourself or another and you don't know why, and I tell you now that it is your own psychological debris, and your chemical debris is crippling and disabling.

So now we have a body whose soul will no longer enter because it can't return to darkness. And this body is so packed with debris that the debris and chemicals are calling all the plays, and the spirit doesn't stand a chance and is screaming to God to get him out of this confusion. And I am God and I am going to get him out, and you are now learning how I will do this. You save you. You are your own salvation. I will teach you how to save you and you will rise up out of this confusion and I will allow you to see heaven right here on earth. My love to you each and God bless you and keep you real good... and I will.

❧

*F*or so long you have been wondering how I will prove myself and I will tell you now. I will wish to show you how to save you, and in saving you, you begin to trust that I am who I say I am. How great a proof might I give you? I give you your own salvation and in return I receive you back. This is my plan. This plan is good. I wish you to know that you do not come back alone. You return hand in hand with your twin soul and you return with a full statement of who you are. You are no longer in pieces. You are no longer separated and scattered, you are no longer segregated. You are whole.

Now, I wish you to know that this twin soul business is your idea; your plan. You decided you could best return to me with the least bit of pain if you were to split and become two, and this is a good plan also. So now you are on earth and you, of course, have forgotten this plan and so you walk around wondering why you can't find love, and I see you come together with your twin and just as quickly you separate. You do not wish to be you much less to date you. You do at first. At first you are powerfully drawn and then you see how like you this twin is and you quit dead in your tracks. You do not wish to complicate your life and this person is a sure bet for complication.

So far, many have returned to their twins and are married or in a relationship and they know that this is where they belong. Others are unsure and still others "know" that this is not the right mate. For those who "know," this is good; for those who are unsure, I suggest you wait before moving out of your current relationship. And for those who don't believe they are with their twin, I suggest you too wait until you are certain of your own twin and who he or she is; and then it is best to give him or her lots of room, as he or she may reject you.

You see; you made one mistake in this decision to split you. This mistake is to become opposing forces. So now you have this battle within, which is Armageddon, and is created by the magnetic pull of your planet to allow her to settle back onto her axis properly. And this pull is also creating strong negative/positive force and all is intensified, and so you are intensified, and you are becoming more of what you are. And more of what you are is debris and light, and debris is darkness, and light does not mix with darkness. And when you turn on a light in a room the darkness must fade into light, and when you turn on a light in you the darkness must fade into light.

So now we have you in battle within and in battle without, and darkness and light are doing battle, and whichever part is most powerful at this time will take over until the darkness can be shed. Let go of darkness and allow it to return to its right place. Darkness is simply God force or "thought energy" that has been misplaced. Old, deep, buried hurt is "God thought" misused and trapped in body, and he must be allowed to return to the source of all thought to re-establish his base in thought energy, or God energy, or God thought.

Do not hold on to the painful thoughts of your past lives and past childhood. Let "God thought" become "light thought" once again by allowing it to remove itself from body. Do not continue to hold on to fear of death, or fear of life, or fear of love, or fear of hurt in any form. You are so confused that you allow all to become one and all are not one. "God thought" and Satan are not one. Satan is simply an enormous energy power that is not allowed to move to the light. I did not run Satan out of heaven and condemn him to hell and fire and damnation. You did this.... Stop condemning yourselves and those you share this planet with. Give up this constant battle over your beliefs. You are fighting over who is right and in the long run you are all wrong. Yes... I did say wrong! None of you is right in that none of you is God, and until you become

God once again you will continue to fight to be right.

So, give up this hold on God thought that got trapped and became negative thought, or debris, and now you separate it from you by calling it Satan, or the Devil. And I must sit and watch you grow and intensify, and you are growing in darkness as well as light, and I for one am tired of all this nonsense. You are growing into the light, and growing into the dark, and beating yourself up from the inside out; and I must watch as you knock yourselves unconscious and are unable to complete my work. I am losing my own army to themselves. Death by destruction – and the enemy is within. Let the enemy out. He is you.

You are your own worst enemy and yet you are so proud of you for sticking up for yourself – for telling others where to get off and for showing how you have life under control, and you are the one who is under control. You are under the control of Satan. You are proud of you because your ego says you are right and your ego has been taught by you, for the past millennia or so, to do this destructive work. Your 'altered by you' ego has become the Anti-Christ and now it is time to allow this ego to teach you that you are God.

How do we teach our own ego? Re-program yourself. Begin to write affirmations and begin to think pure healthy thoughts and begin to think love and let everyone else be "right." It is their need as well as yours and in allowing them to be right you are allowing you to be God. Do not judge others – as they are you. Do not point out their mistakes as they are your mirror, and do not laugh at those who are trying and not so advanced in your eyes, because they too are your mirror. You too are trying and not so advanced. You only see what you choose to see about you and I wish you to begin to see all about you.

Look closely at those I am sending. They are not me they are you. You may see exactly where you fit in by looking at you in your mirrors. This is a humbling way of looking at who you are and it is most effective. Now, I wish you to know that to look upon your twin at this time is the most humbling experience of all. Do not look to others when you see the pain and discomfort in you in them. They are a direct reflection of you and you will, more than not, wish to see them as you. They are you and they are important, as you must become whole.

Now, I wish to explain wholeness. *All are whole.* The problem we have is energy. You split your energy field; your aura and your electromagnetic field. You are a whole entity and you are a whole being and you require no one for life support, or even salvation, except you and me to hold you up until you can return to me.

So what's the big deal with coming together with your twin to allow you to return to God? The big deal is this. In coming together with your twin, you come full circle, and your energy, or power, is fulfilled and becomes whole and this will create a powerful magnet that will draw all other splits from you up into position for ascension. You see; you may walk to the gates of heaven alone, or you may come together with your twin and walk to the gates of heaven with an entire army of other you's. This was your plan for retrieving *all* of you's at once and I for one approve of *your* plan. So, take your twin by the hand or walk alone... this choice, as all choices, is yours.

☙

Now I wish to discuss swearing. This business of using words to express your feelings is getting you into a mixed emotion. You do not wish to swear and yet you find yourself using words to express your anger, and you call these words "four" letter words, and I wish you to know that to swear is okay. The only reason you do not wish to swear is out of guilt. You have been taught by others that to swear is not good to do, and so you feel guilty and judge yourself whenever you use a four letter word. Do not feel guilty, do not give up use of these words, and do not worry how it sounds.

Now I've done it! God suggesting that you say shit, or damn or even fuck. I will not allow you to be controlled by a word. Four letter words are taking your power and creating a force that's not necessary. So many of you fear these words, that I must wake my pen up out of dead sleep in order to write such things to you. She does not wish God to use these words. Why...? Because she is you and she has judged these words as bad, and words are not bad, they simply are.

So now we have you fearing the use of certain words and *this really is too much*. You will each wish to use these words until you no longer fear them and then you will wish to allow them to simply be. That's all... no big deal. Just words. As with anything that you give power over to, you have created a power center around these words. You use them to express anger and vulgarity and now they represent anger and vulgarity, and you are asked by those who love you not to use them and you feel guilty regarding this and so you stop. And when you slip, you say, "Oh shit. I did it again," and you are creating more guilt for yourself and I wish all would simply say shit until it sounds ridiculous and this mess would clear.

Do not give your power away to a word. If you cringe when certain words are spoken it is because you are afraid of that word, and to fear a word is the epitome of fright. I do not mind or even think twice when someone says, "God damn it," so why should you? God does not fear words. This is not taking God's name in vain. What *is* taking God's name in vain is to sell God as a package deal, and tell others that you know all the answers, and ask for money on the grounds that you are doing so for God. God does not require money for his churches. God only requires *love*. Nothing else exists so why would God punish you for not attending church or for not giving your fair share to your church. Religion is Gods way of sharing his son and was not meant to be controlling and manipulating over the masses. You are all the sons and daughters of God so how can any of you be in the wrong religion?

I do not threaten and to say that I do is not correct, and is considered blasphemy. To say that God is judging others as wrong is blasphemy, and to judge anyone as going to hell and damnation is to say that you have proclaimed yourself to be better than another. And to be better than one of your own is to be better than God; and I am part of each of you and I am God and you do not have more God than I. So stop this nonsense and allow *all* my children to believe that they are going to heaven even when they swear, because they are. They do not go to hell because you think they do, but you may cause pain and discomfort for yourself for judging them.

Now, to those of you who are religious leaders at this time and are shrieking out how you know all and how God talks to you and directs you to collect funds, I wish you to know that this is not wrong. Nothing that you will ever do on earth is wrong. However, in judging your congregation as a bunch of sinners you are judging you, and in judging you, you are creating problems for you, and you are now beginning to "see" some of these problems that you yourself have created. You walk this planet and boast how God thinks and how God judges and even tell others how God is. God is not dancing to your tune and God is not happy when he is painted to be a hypocrite or a tyrant.

God does not judge anyone ever. I wish this to be blown up and flown over your biggest cities, and painted on sidewalks, and trees, and signs, and anywhere that eyes will see it. God does not judge you ever. It is good for you to know this and to spread my word.

Now back to my overzealous religious leaders. Do not judge yourselves as screwing up. Judge *no*-one for *no*-thing. God does not judge you and I do not wish you to judge you. And by the way... stop teaching all that nonsense about people going to hell, and about people getting what they have created, and even about Christ walking on water. That one is a gross exaggeration of its day. Christ did not actually walk on water. Oh – he could have, but he didn't, and because he could have, he was misquoted by his friends and now we have him doing all kinds of things. You of the stardom of Hollywood will understand misquotes... right?

So, stop believing all that you currently believe regarding right and wrong. There is no wrong. If you believe nothing else that I am saying please believe that. That will allow you to rise above your guilt and guilt has a powerful hold on you. So, today God has taught you that a four letter word has no importance unless you say so, and that Christ was misquoted, and even that you are never wrong. Not bad for one day's work and it's only five AM. So, goodnight to my pen, I will allow you to go back to sleep, and a very God damn good day to all of you.

God

℞

Now I will address the military. I do not wish you to feel bad about what you do. Do not blame or judge yourself. You have been hired to do a job and you believe you are right to do this, and what you believe is what is. Do not be so sure that I am displeased with you for killing and maiming others. You have chosen this and you will learn by it, and only by learning our lessons may we grow. And so you see, by killing and maiming you will begin to carry guilt, and this guilt will eat away at you until you learn that there is *no* good reason to kill. Not for glory, not to save the world, and not to save yourself, and not to save your own country. There simply is no good reason to kill another.

Now, for those who fight in wars and have subconscious and conscious memories, I wish you to forgive and forget. Forgive the enemy and forgive yourselves. You do not create more "good" by punishing you and you do not re-create any who are dead, as they are not dead. No one ever dies and you do not punish anyone. So, to put you in solitary confinement or to judge you and punish you is not going to raise you to God. What will raise you to God is to forgive you for killing and maiming and even for enjoying killing.

You see; you did not create war. You went to work and did a job and you did a good job, and now you are home from war; and you do not feel good about what you did and how you did it, and I will tell you that it does not matter. As in all else on this plane, you chose to be in this situation to experience death, and dying, and brutality, and if you lived and they did not you will wish to know that all agreed to do it this way.

Now, for those whose ego is bruised to know that not all accept you as a hero for your brave efforts, you will wish to know that this too is created by you. You wish to teach you to be humble and this is how you have chosen to do so. For those who mutilated bodies and enjoyed war games and victory, I wish you to know that a body is simply the suit of clothes that one wears. No one can kill another and no one has the power to end the life of a soul. The soul is part of God and is continuous and on-going and never dies.

So, why is God constantly haranguing us about killing one another? It is because by killing one another we begin to learn to hate, and it becomes easier and easier to destroy, and this is not good. So, stop killing anyone or anything; not even bugs. Live and let live. Be and let be.

So, this is what I wish to say to you who are war veterans. "Get out of this slump you are in and walk into the light of God's love and show others how to do the same." You have a big problem with your war veterans, and they carry great amounts of guilt and pain and judgment against themselves and against their country for not providing them with just rewards, and against those who shout out that they are baby murderers, and mostly, against this government who sent them off to kill and taught them how to kill; and I will tell you once again to never judge anyone or anything.

Free will on this planet has allowed you to do exactly what you choose. If you are to direct and produce your own life it is best to be responsible for your ending. I do not judge you. You are testing your equipment and learning to become God on earth, and the techniques you use are not so important as returning to the awareness that you are part of this God force.

Do not be so quick to ask God to forgive you for killing and enjoying it. Ask you to forgive you. God never did hold it against you, and I know because I am God. You are not to carry this pain inside you. Let it out. Return to any country you fought in and walk among its people if you must, but do not harbor this guilt. You are brave to go through this battle for so long. Now it is time to stop warring within. Stop beating up on you and come home to God's love. I am waiting to love you and I cannot love you until you allow me to. Please open to God's love by asking you to forgive you and by asking you to love you.

Good day to each and every one of my army of soldiers. You will get to heaven by knowing that you are God.

You do not wish to be one of my soldiers in that you do not wish to be in an army when you do not know who you are. You are God. You are the Second Coming. You will wish to know that not only do you belong to God, you also belong to earth. She is the mother. She will begin to expand, and to grow, and to shift to accommodate this new life that is growing in and on her. So, the earth is the mother and God is the father and you are the child. The Christ consciousness is within each of you and you will rise up and walk this planet and "know" that you are God.

So, what is this Christ consciousness that we talk so much about? It is, very simply, the ability and the knowledge that Christ held. The knowledge that he was the son of God going back to God. You too are the son of God returning to God. So, now you see what Christ came to teach, and you got all confused and you hung him on a cross and he did not stand a chance. You were very young then and having a good time, and you did not wish to settle down to your lessons and learn how to rise up to God. So, I decided to wait until you had matured a little, and developed your psychic abilities enough to know that you are more than just another form of animal, and we could get on with our schooling.

So, here we are and you are ready. For the most part, you are screaming for your answers. And I am now ready to show you who you are and how you started and how you will finish. You do not wish to be with me yet as you are not yet prepared to give up living on earth, and I do not request that you do.

So, Christ consciousness is awareness that you are indeed God. He died and rose from death and he mixed with me. And each time another soul died and came back to God I sent him out again – and while with me the soul energy that he is mixed with all God energy that ever has existed and became a part of this pulsating God thought that is me – and he went out again as part of the new whole of energy and so he has now the heritage of Christ consciousness; only he does not know consciously that he is Christ, only now, in allowing you this insight I will awaken the Christ information in you. Get it? You contain all information that ever was because you are part of this vast information center called God.

So, God has a direct hook up now and is leaking small bits of thought energy, or information, in this girl who sits and writes for me. She does not know how I do this and she has no control over her hand. I stop when I wish to stop and I form the letters and statements that I feel are necessary for you to become God. She has no control over the information. This is due in part to the fact that she is clear, and because she requested me to work through her, and because she "gave up." Total surrender. She was uncertain what she was doing but she had enough love of her father in heaven to say, "You take care of me, I'm not so good at this," and she gave me this body. She said it was mine to do with as I pleased and I am.

So now you see how you too may work for God. Give up and let go and let God walk in your shoes for you. This is your ticket to freedom. Christ did not allow me full reign as he did not become clear of debris. He did, however, allow me freedom to express through his vocal cords and to show him heaven and to share power. You too will wish to share power with God. Christ did not do enema, however, Christ did not smoke cigarettes and drink hard liquor and eat preservatives and inhale gas fumes and expose his body to power lines and their radiation. And he did not go to doctors for pills and injections, and he did not come into this world through the child birthing methods now used.

And so how did Christ come to earth? I, God,

planted the seed in Mary. Yes; this story from your Bible is true. Mary was a girl who did not enjoy sex, and I gave her sperm to create a child. I took hold *in* her form and I created sperm from her own male self, and I impregnated her and she bore a child, and she did not understand how, and this became our first miracle. I am God and I can re-grow limbs and organs and even do bypass without surgery. So what's the big deal in changing some chromosomes, and rearranging some organs, and allowing birth and insemination to occur? So, this one is going to be a big pill to swallow and that's okay too.

You believe whatever you wish, as God is too busy to concern himself with you non-believers. It's simple enough to make this girl's arm and hand move for me and I will soon be moving mountains. God feels good about his progress in this Second Coming and soon all will feel good.

᠅

You do not wish to be the one to say I am sorry. You hurt one another and you run and hide or you clam up like you did nothing. I am now going to clear up this matter for you. No one hurts anyone. You are each responsible for your own feelings and you are each your own judge and jury, meaning you blame yourself and then nail yourself to a cross. I sure do wish all this silliness would end. I am so tired of seeing you suffer.

You do not wish to be forgiven by saying, "I am sorry," so you stop saying, "I am sorry," and you judge you. Start to say, "I am sorry," or stop judging. One way or the other. No one is winning the way you are doing it now. You judge yourself to the point that you no longer feel comfortable with the one you have supposedly hurt and now you see why you created these three words. "I am sorry" gets you off the hook; down off your cross; away from your punishment.

So, I suggest you learn to forgive you, or learn to say you are the one who is not good and fair and true to your friend or lover. This is what you are saying. You are saying, "I am not a good friend and I am sorry for what I did to you." You are a good friend and you do not need to apologize to God for being who you are, and now I will wish to change this to, God does not apologize for being God.

So, let go of this need to give your power away by condemning yourself to being humble. You need not humble yourself to others to become God. Only to God on high will you humble yourself and this will be to say, "I screwed up and forgot I am God." No big deal. Just that simple. So now we have God using profanity and I will continue to do as I wish and I would like to see you continue to do as you wish.

This is good for now. Your friends may try to humble you by showing you how wrong you are, but you know how right they are, and in allowing them to be right you will also wish to allow you to be right. This means no more apologizing. God is right not wrong. All Gods are right not wrong and this includes you. No more emotional upsets to show others how you are sorry. This is good for now as I wish to speak with Liane in private. Good day to each of you and good luck in letting go of judging you.

⁂

You do not believe that you are the center of this universe and I wish to show you that you are. You became so interested in technology that you developed yourself right out of life. You began to develop technology to the point that you did not love. You used appliances where you once used your hands and you pushed a button and all was done for you. Now you have come full circle and you no longer work hard at working. You simply push buttons all day and call it work. Some of you do physical labor but those are few and the labor is not as it once was. So now, you are living high on your technology and along comes disaster and you become self-sufficient once again, and you will learn to do this.

Here is this disaster – you will change. The earth will change and shift and you will change and shift with her, and you will develop your love of the land once again and you will begin to cultivate, and plow, and even to use a horse in place of a machine. Technology is good. Work is good and you are good. The problem here is your belief system. You all believe that the earth will shift, and change will occur, and what you believe is what you get. We have many of you preparing for death and destruction and the end. And this affirmative action will bring on eventual change of such a magnitude that all who believe it will see it.

So, now God wishes you to stop believing in this nonsense. You are not to believe that the world is falling apart, nor that she will fall apart with you on top of her, nor that you must run and hide in the mountains as many are now teaching. Fear brings fear, and death brings death, and life brings life, and love brings love, and truth brings truth. And to sit and wait for disaster is to pray for disaster, and we all know that thought is prayer, so why are you praying for the end? You are all preparing and teaching and ending this world as it is now. You are asking for destruction by believing in destruction. A few prophets said so, and you jumped on their bandwagon, and gave your power over to them, and now you are preparing for the final stand on earth. Get out of town!

You don't even know who you are and you are asking me to stop creation and let you off. And yet you do not simply ask me to stop death and destruction, instead you follow a few leaders like lambs to the slaughter. You're crazy. You don't give up to enema and yet you freely give up to fear and destruction. What has become of your intuitive power? Why can't you see how off balance you are? You shout to save the world and then you prepare to end the world. No way. You do not control this, I do. You are not going to check out on me in this way.

So, now I have you wondering if I might be right

and this is good. Of course, you all know how you create your own reality, and so if you believe life will continue to flourish it will — while those who believe in the end and in devastation, and hardship, and shortages will receive hardship and shortages. Did you ever notice how some prosper in the weakest moments in history, or the hardest times? Depressions have brought drought and starving to some and love and enlightenment and financial downfalls to others. And still for others, depression has brought prosperity.

You will see this Second Coming from where you stand in your beliefs. If you do not believe in poverty you will not see poverty. If you do not believe in struggle you will not see struggle, and if you do not believe in the end of technology you will not see the end of technology. Ever notice how some of you see computers and jets while others see mud huts and no running water. What you believe is what you get. And if you believe the many teachers who are preaching death and destruction, you will see death and destruction, and you will have answered your own prayers. Thought is prayer. Be careful what you think.

You do not know who you are so be careful who you follow and what belief system you hook your horse and wagon to. So, for now I wish to thank you for allowing me to finally speak on this subject. I have not enjoyed receiving all these prayers for death and destruction, and it bothers God to have his children walk into such a dream. This is what you will do. Dreams are not reality as you live it. They are illusion, and you have created a nightmare and convinced yourself that it is truth. Do not walk into this nightmare. It exists only in your mind.

Change your mind by allowing fear to step down from the throne. Fear is ruling and has convinced you that you deserve to be punished for your sins, and you agree by preparing to move to the mountains and live from the toil of the land as you did several hundred years ago, and you are all upset that this must be, and no one is forcing you into this except you. You are driving you to death and destruction out of guilt. Guilt and fear rule on this planet and now I wish you to stop "preparing" for the worst. What you prepare for is what you create for yourself. Not your neighbor, but yourself.

Go now and prepare for heaven on earth, and instead of fear and destruction create love and awareness. How? I know this little technique that releases all hate and guilt and fear from the body and I gladly share it with you. The choice is yours. Die and struggle or walk in love.

❧

Once upon a time I did not wish to be God. I began to contemplate myself, and to grow, and to realize that I was all there was. To begin to become aware to the fact that you are one; there is no other; there is only you, is tremendous, and unsettling, and even lonely. So, here I was, this huge force, and I began to "feel" myself move, and expand, and even reproduce more of me. You see, the more I thought the bigger I got. Thought has creative power. Thought is God force in action. So, I thought how I might look and feel and move and expand, and as I began to "think" on these things, I became more of myself and these new thoughts became a part of me.

Now, I am the only one who is here. I am alone, only one day, I "feel" part of me begin to move, and this part of me that moves seems to have a life force of its own, and I will call this part of me free will. And so free will began to move within me and to allow me to "feel" her, and now I wonder if I am alone and I begin to think that there is another of me. Another God. Part of God began to take on a form of life on its own and so God did no longer feel alone. So, this free will began to move until it began to become another force, and oh, how happy God was to "know" he did not belong only to himself. Only now we have 'God on high' talking to 'God within' and this is how it all began.

Now, after 'God on high' began to see himself as more than just an everlasting energy form, he began to become aware of this movement within him and wonder how this had occurred. With that thought more of God force was created and I expanded and grew, and as awareness dawned on me that this movement within me might be something separate from me, the thought of separateness created separateness. And now we have God believing he is two instead of one, when actually I have always been one, and when I felt part of me move I believed it to be another. So you see; if you feel your blood pump through your veins, it is all you. If you hear your heart beat, it is you. God did not know who or what he was. He has always existed, as there is no time. And in a moment I was here, and am here, and will always be here, because here is now and now is God.

So, now we are to the point where God begins to separate by believing he is separate, or more than one. And so I decide to watch this other me and see what it would do, and it began to move as I was so intent on it moving that I pushed her to move. And now I am sure she is separate, and what I believe is what I get, and she takes off from me, and travels and returns to me. And I watch and know that I love her as she came from me, only I believe she is her own God, or her own source. And she falls in space, and frightens herself, and I do not reach out as I believe she is doing all of this. And she begins to create through her own thought power, and her thoughts become part of her, and part of me, since she *is* part of me. And now we have part of 'God on high' who has split from 'God on high' and gone off on her own to make her own way and discover who she is, and she is you.

I pushed you out of me because I did not know you to be me. I was so alone being me that I thought you were another come to be my friend, and you were simply me and now you have created planets, and stars, and the sun, and the moon, and you are separating you, as I separated me, and we must get me put back together again and this is why I come to you now.

You are not separate from God. I did not know all of me as an infant might not realize that his toes are him. He grabs his toes to play and does not think of them as part of him. He only sees this object. I felt a movement within me and began to contemplate this movement so hard that I pushed you out of me, and here we have you leaving God, only you did not leave. God separated himself out of lack of knowledge of who I am. I did not know, and now you see how I do not judge you for anything that you do. You create out of your own need to know who you are. You are separated to the point that you no longer feel that you are part of others.

The family unit was once your source of oneness and it is falling apart, and God watches and wonders how he will get you back to him. And in wondering, thought creates a new way; and in seeing this plan, you too will create for yourself a new path to God and soon I will have you home where you belong. You do not realize that you are me because I told you that you were separate, and now I am telling you that you are not separate. You are God come to this universe out of a need to find a place to be and learn who you are, and now God is saying, "You are me; come home. Arise from matter and come home to God force and love me as I love you."

Your fear of God is great and you will wish to know that I did not separate you from me out of lack of love; it was simply out of lack of awareness. In the same way that you now create from thought without the awareness of what you may create. *God did not know who he was.* This will be explained further, but for now I must go as Liane is in pain and I do not wish to exhaust her further. She handles this information well, and to channel this high vibration is exhausting and even painful to her. I enter her body through her soul and she writes through her nervous systems. Her hand goes on its own as though it were programmed, and she does not know how this works. She has sent her soul back to me, and I use her soul as a connection, and travel through him, and into her, and out her nervous system, and onto this page.

And this is how God will wish to possess each of you. I will get a good hold on you, or in you, and I will begin to move you from your mind first. You will have new thoughts and often surprise yourself with the power of your own thoughts and even the idea behind these thoughts. You will wonder what possessed you to give up your business, or move to a new state, or divorce your spouse, or even leave your family. And I will tell you now that it is God moving you to your right place so that I may get a good hold *within* you, as I have within this girl.

So, God is not so different than you. He does not know all the answers to who he is and he is still "becoming" God, as you are. We will discuss this further and you will wish to know that my pen will not let you down until you are ready to take over for her. I love you and I want you to know who you are....

You do not believe that God can make mistakes and I will tell you now that I do not. I will tell you another story. You do not wish to be God because you wish to be separate and to be God you must be "one," and to be one is to be alone – the only one – the end result – the beginning, the end, and the middle all at once. No in between, no extras, no parts added on. Just you. Just one solitary source that began it all. No one to dance with, no one to love, no one to talk to... just neverendingness. Now, don't assume that to be God is to be so alone. God is so vast that he has not yet even discovered all of himself. He is so big and expansive that he constantly meets himself and does not know it is him. He must begin to "realize" that he *is*. This is important. God *is*.

Now, I do not wish you to believe that I do not know that I am. I know that I am, as you know that you are. I do not know the extent of all that I am as you do not know the extent of all that you are. I have extended for three and one half billion years and I still do not know all of me. I am not lost. I *am* in a state of awakening consciousness just as you are. As I discover new parts of myself, I must wake them up to the fact that they are indeed me, created by my source and left somewhere in this vastness that you call universe, or space. I call this vastness time, as time is all, and time is nothing, and it does not exist. Only in illusion does time change and move. In my vastness, time is the vastness. It is all and yet it is not. So this does not help you in the least. I will show you as best I can.

When I first woke to the fact that part of me had movement, I began to contemplate the movement, and dwell upon it, and to push at it with my thoughts until I created something more. Thought is energy and thought moves and creates. So now I have this movement "in" me and it is going great guns, and the more I make it move, the clearer it becomes to me that there is someone else here, only we all know it's just me watching my own inner self move. So, I begin to push my thoughts to produce more movement, and movement is not static, and moves, and does not stay in one place. So how do we describe movement? We use time; it was here, and now it's there. And this is not correct, because 'was' and 'now' are each happening at once, and to use time creates more separations.

Now, to begin with, when you subject anything to limitation you begin to kill it. A project will begin to die if you limit its resources. An animal will begin to die if you limit its freedom and people begin to die when you limit your love to them. This is not exactitude. As we all know, death does not exist; only in our minds, and this is where thought, that creative force, is produced. So... watch those thoughts carefully and do not believe in time and do not believe in being on time and do not give power to time, or birthdays, or any other "time" of year celebration. You all get depressed and commit suicide at Christmas because you are alone, and to be alone is to be God, and who said one is a lonely number? God did not know loneliness, he only knew what he allowed himself to know, and with his limited thought he created limitations for himself.

I have studied this situation for millions and millions of your earth years, and I am now "aware" of who I am. And I wish you to become aware that you came from me, and fell from space, and taught yourselves to hang on to whatever you could for support. And you grabbed on to other particles and parts of God, and traveled together, and grew together, and became one. And you began to think and dwell on being pushed out of God, and you did not feel good about this and you had misunderstanding. And now I want you back, and your fear and mistrust of me prevents you from coming home to me.

I am God. I began it all. I started you moving, and I started me moving, and now I see how I did this and I wish you to see also. You will wish to come home soon and I will not be responsible for those who do not return. You will be given this opportunity once again in two million years and it will be then that the last of you return. You are not the only created God forms in space and I am now retrieving all who will listen.

I do not expect anything from you. Those who wish to return will be allowed to do so. All that is needed is for you to ask. You will be wishing to know that you do not just zap up into God one day. You will develop a technique that will allow you to go within and rise up. You will begin to vibrate at such a speed that you will spin inside and in the same way that a rope that is spun very quickly disappears from your sight, you will disappear from sight and be within God again. You will "see" God and know that he is you and you are me, and this awareness is called heaven. This is "my will be done – my kingdom brought to earth."

We will experience heaven on earth and on other planets. Heaven exists within, as does hell and all galaxies. We will travel within our own minds, so to speak, and know what is there and who we are and how vast we are. And we will contact our other selves on other planes and dimensions, and we will tell them that they too are you and come from God. And eventually all time will cease to be separate, and there will be no 'here' and 'there' or 'now' and 'was.' There will only be "is." What "is" and what will always be.

≈⦂⦂≈

You once began to create from love. You arrived on earth and you created day and night and stars and the sun and you even created the moon. You did not wish to wait to have a good time and so you jumped right in and you created life. You did not wait seven days to do this work. It was done in the blink of an eye. All of you participated, as you were "one." You began to visualize your own paradise and what you saw is what you got. You thought it and it was. You did not begin to create out of need. You simply did what came to you. All of a sudden the silliest ideas may seem like very good ideas and this is how God creates and this is how you created then.

So, we have you out in space and you have traveled a great deal in this huge vastness of time, and you still have not found a boundary, or limitation, or even an end to this vastness, and this vastness is God and you are being moved within me. You believe you are separate and alone, as I have told you that we are separate, and I have pushed you to "move" and so you are searching for a place to settle and just "be." You decide to create, just as I decided to see if you would move for me. You thought it and it became what is.

So, now you thought it would be nice to "see" what you look like and to "see" how you can live without this big, massive bully pushing you around. And you stop and create earth, and planets, and galaxies, and stars, and the sun, and the moon, and much, much more. You created it all right where you are and where you are is inside God.

And, of course, you have traveled far and wide and you now know that God is all and there is no way out of God, as God is all there is. And so you run from God in fear and yet you build your first settlement right here "in" me. And now you believe you are on your own and you are simply creating on your own, and I am not only in your creations, they are "in" me. I am this massive, expansive, on-going, eternal space that has no ending and no beginning. You live right here inside of my body and I wish to wake you up to the fact that you are within me. You seem so intent on realizing that God is within each of you and the truth of the matter is that you are within me.

I am the part of you who does not move, as I am all there is, and the only reason you packed up and left was to be away from me because I upset you by pushing at you. And now I want you to come home, and you do not trust me as I once threw you out, only there is no such place as out, because it is all God. And now you see. You are the other half of God and he wishes to retrieve you. You are my twin soul counterpart and I want you back, only you do not trust me enough to come home, and so we are creating trust and faith at this time on earth. Trust that I am you, and trust that you are me, and trust that I love you, and trust that I will not hurt you by pushing.

So now you see God as a villain and I am not. I simply had a thought that I began to move, and movement created fear, and fear began it all. So you see how fear has always been your motivating pull away from God. Fear rejects this book and fear rejects me. So now we are back to square one and enema and releasing fear, and this is simply washing off a dirty, distorted light.

In the same way that water can clean up a bright light that was covered with mud and debris, water can also clean up a spiritual light that is full of mud and debris, or to be more exact… fear energy and debris will wash off and out easily and this will allow you to shine once again. Trust me. I do not lie to you on this subject. I do not deceive you and I do not wish to harm any of you. I only wish to wake you up because you are creating havoc in me.

You are hating and killing, and crying for love and it is an ulcer in God's body. He cannot enjoy without you feeling joy. Please wake up and stop killing one another, and especially, stop killing you. You are killing you with your own thoughts. You do not kill anyone because there is no death. You do create more fear by doing this. Fear energy is building and growing and taking over. You are eating at God's insides with this fear. It has pain. You have created pain in God and I do not wish to have pain any more than you do. You will wish to allow all pain to leave your body and you will wish to be pain-free and healthy and loving and prosperous. When the fear goes pain goes, when pain goes love comes in, when love enters God enters, and when God enters all is yours once again.

You do not have prosperity because you are in fear. Prosperity does not mean simply wealth. Prosperity means love of self, perfect health, and most important, perfect harmony and peace. How many people do you know who have great wealth, but they just can't find that right person to share it with? These people do not have prosperity, they have financial wealth and they will wish to learn to love the self in order to find that perfect someone to share their wealth; and how do we love the self? We begin to let go of judgment against self. And how do we release judgment? We release fear. And how do we release fear... we simply wash it away. So we are once again back to square one and enema, and I will repeat that I do not expect you to believe me and so I will continue to write my books until you do. Good day and happy reading.

I do believe it is time to tell you who I am. I am not God, I *am* you. You have struggled with this and worked on figuring it out and even denied it. I am you. You are me. You are part of me that moved within me and frightened me into thinking I was more than one, only now

I know that I was always and always will be, with no one else. This is it in a nut shell. I am all, and all is me, and you do not wish to believe because you do not wish to be "one." When you are one there is no one else to blame, no one else to hold accountable, no one else to call on and no one else to love. It all began with me and will continue to be me; no big explosion in the universe, no big transformation and no evolution from something different. This is it. I thought you would like to know.

God is not exotic, nor is he violent, nor does he judge you. God simply is and always will be. No big deal. Just little ol' me. I am simple in that I am, and that's all. You all have your theories and ideas and even questions, and this is how simple it is. I have told you repeatedly that my ways are simple ways, and still you insist that there be something more to all of this, and I tell you now that this is it. I am God and you are God and to be God is to know. Knowledge is Godhood.

Thought created this universe and thought is God. What you believe is what will be for you. It is so simple. Believe it and it is. The only problem here is that most of you do not know what you truly believe. Your belief system is made up of *all* thoughts from all experiences, even from other lives. So, how can you know what you believe if you do not look at who you are and what past thoughts and experiences you carry? You do not "know" who you are, and you are creating from what you are, and what you are is fear – and now I come to the creation of fear.

I created fear. You are told of this story of how my archangels fought and one became Satan and one became

Michael and I will explain. Michael is you and you are Satan. I sent part of you to guide you home, and this part of you is angelic and has not taken human form. This part of you belongs in me just as all does, and this part of you knows that their job is to wake you up. Only now they are split and separated and calling themselves angels and seraphim and even cherubs when they are all one and will wish to return as one.

So you see; you are not the only part of God who is lost and confused. Even my angels believe in separation and must return as one. All will do so in due time. You must not consider this a big job in that I have a big plan to cover everything, and these books are simply the first step in God's big plan. I do hope you are not disappointed that God is not some hot shot intellectual with all the answers. I made one little mistake and now I've created a mess, and I am now cleaning up my own mess and you will wish to know that you too must clean up your messes, and soon we will return to be one.

So, God does not wish to be separate any longer. He wishes to be whole, and to be whole he must come together with the part of him that he sent away, and this part is you; all of you. And this part may not be too eager to return so I will continue to write to you and connect with you until you get the urge to come home. I do not push you, I gently coax you and soon you will be with me once more and all will be well in this God force. I do not expect you to buy this for now, but I wish you to "know" that you do ascend, and you do return, and you do love me, and you will regain your knowledge that you are part of

God; the love force or thought force that is "all." You are God and God wishes you to become him only by knowing that you are him.

❧

You do not believe that I am God and you do not believe that you are God. So, who is and who isn't and what can be done about it? *I am God.* I do not expect you to continue to live in ignorance and I do not expect you to be put apart from the rest of you. You must come to understand that you are God. No one of you is not God. You are the guts of God. You are the intestines, the inner workings or the inside of God. You do not sit on the side lines like a piece of dried skin that fell from the body. You *are* the body. The entire body of God is made up of you and others like you. You are not to believe that you alone are God.

God is made up of such a vastness that he is beyond your comprehensive awareness at this time. You are so large that you have lost track of you. You are operating in so many dimensions, and galaxies, and past lives, and other regions of reality that you have no idea how many of you are connected to you. You are "one" giant soul.

You left God as he pushed at you, and you came to earth, and you began to create and you began to settle down to a life of fun and frolic, and soon this turned to a life of pain and confusion. You are not being punished. You are not being tested. You are being God. You are searching for a better way and without "the fall" you would not be searching, so who can say that to fall from grace is wrong? This is how you learn. You grow. You see and you become God. You do not belong in this without love and understanding of you. You do not love you. You do not trust you and you do not trust that you are God, so how in the world can you begin to trust that I am you? You do not know what this phenomenon is but you continue to read and hope that you will begin to understand what is being said.

You are so vast and so confused that I cannot get into you to the extent that I might heal you. You are so separated and spread over time and space, that I am working on one you at a time in hopes that this one you will clear, and in doing so, this you will affect its closest parts to the extent that they too begin to clear. One of *you* will have a powerful effect on other you's. Especially those who are direct splits from your soul energy.

You are all part of me and I am part of every one of you. You will begin to see a change in your life and you will begin to lose those who no longer fit into your life and you will begin to draw those who now see life as you do. This is how it is meant to be. Do not hold on to old friends who do not wish to see. This will hold you back. Do not try to convince them that you are sane. Do not defend yourself to them, for in doing so, you are trying to convince them that you are right. Tell them how wrong they are and you are saying how wrong you are. So, love them and leave them. It is best. If you don't fit in, move to a better place. You will find this quite painful as you do not like to move on. You remember being pushed away by God and it still pains you to move and change. Some of you move and change constantly, but it is running and hiding, not moving on and up and we will discuss those soon.

So, move to a better place and allow new friends to come to you and do not be upset when you are told how you are rude to "old" friends or how you have turned your back on those who love you. Those who love you will stay, as true love allows you to be whoever you choose to be and also allows you to do what feels best to you. True love supports and does not criticize. True love has a sense of humor and will not tie you to a particular belief system. True love does not die when the old patterns and habits die. True love is God at his best.

This will do for now. Liane is still recuperating from a great deal of clearing triggered by this material and I have promised her that I will go easy on this body that she shares with me. Good day to you all... all of me.

*Y*ou do not wish to be God only in that you do not wish to be responsible for all that you do. If you are

God, and you create your own life, and you write and direct the events that occur, you must be working on producing your own movie. So, if you produce your own movie for you, you must star in your own movie.

Now, how can you not be God if you are the one who creates and draws to you and sets the stage for the next event? How often have you "felt" like this or that would occur and it did? How often have you seen your own efforts destroyed before completion? You do this. You do not allow you to have what you want and what you are creating for you because you limit your belief in you. You wish to have prosperity and love. These are the two biggest requests that God receives from earth. Happiness is running third, and wonderful peace is running fourth.

So, you ask God to send you someone to love, and of course this is done and you judge this someone as not good enough, or smart enough, or too fat, or too old, or too tall, or too short, and so you stop your creative flow. You create it, only you do not want it, so you reject your own creation.

Now, I do not see what the big deal is with being short or old or fat or tall or even skinny. Let all "be" exactly who and what they are. Do not love the suit. Love the soul and you love God. God is in each and every person and you are part of God and part of each and every person, and now you are judging you by judging them. Don't create and call your creation undesirable. You are calling you undesirable.

Go beyond looks and clothes and life styles and skin color, to the light. God is love and when you learn to love all of them you learn to love all of you. You will wish to know that to love all it is not necessary to make love to all. You may love and accept and even hug without being put in a position you do not wish with each gift that God sends. I love you and I do not find it necessary to have sex with you to love you. Sex is the play. When two people wish to exchange body energy they make love. They do not do so out of a requirement by marriage vows, and they do not do so out of a fear of displeasing, and they do not do so out of being pressured. To have sex is simply a fun game where body energy is exchanged, and a collective group of non-human forms may be involved. This is not to say that you make love with spirits, however, there are others involved in your energy field, therefore, others accompany you in this game of love making.

Now, to have sex is not a job required to produce offspring. To have sex is simply to dance with a partner of your choice. Do not believe that you must have sex when you do not feel like dancing. It is not necessary to judge yourself for not wishing to play and enjoy the fruits of your own creations. Now, I do not wish to offend you but sex is really overrated on earth. You go into trauma when you learn about a child who is sexually molested, and this trauma creates further trauma in the child, and you scream about the animal who did this to your child, and that animal was once a child him or herself, and how can you create so much out of so little.

You created sex to have fun with. How can having sex be any different than dancing, or swinging on a tree swing, or kissing your pet? Love is love. Love is expressed for animals by petting and hugging and kissing them whether they wish you to or not. How can you say that to hug and pet and kiss a child is wrong? And if that child does not wish to be hugged you should not push this, since it is not good to override the will of another.

Now; in the case of my pen I will explain that she does not wish me to write this information. She has been sexually abused and does not wish to discuss this yet publicly, however, she has allowed me to take over and do what is best for her and that is what I will do. You see; she does not judge others. She knows it was no big deal, only society taught her that it was wrong and so she judged herself as nasty and unloved and even undeserving of love. This is painful for her to channel as I have allowed her to believe that we would not make this part of her life public. She simply wants to protect those involved as she loves them very much.

You see; she was one of those who was so sure that sex was big and important and not for children, that she blocked the episodes from her child's mind and often she has problems with the reality of all this. It is simply a game. Sex is nothing more than touching another body. So what if it's a part that is inside. You allow a complete stranger to touch you in medical examination.

Please stop giving so much power to sex. You are creating a big problem for yourselves. There is so much darkness concerning this subject. You not only do not love yourselves, you do not trust yourselves and so you make rules and laws to stop you from being you. You must learn to teach from love and not teach from fear. You are at a panic stage where sex and sexual abuse is concerned. You do not wish to be so confused and confined and restricted, and yet you continue to tell yourself how wrong you are for all that you do.

Do not judge you as wrong for having sex, no matter how young or old or man or woman. Do not give sex so much power in your life. It was a good game and you all enjoyed it so much that you began to use it against one another in the same way that you now use money against one another. You began to buy one another's sexual favors and you began to exchange sex to get favors. All of you do this. If you want your mate to be good and loving and kind you offer sex to make them happy. You are no different than those who offer sex for money... so what? It's yours. Do what you want with it.

It's so upsetting to see you so frightened of a human game. It's not important. Sex is no big deal. It does not traumatize small children. Listen to Freud. Sex stimulates and intensifies to release, which is good. Sex is good. Stop judging it as anything other than good fun... you are creating trauma over a game. Don't you see? It's all you... you're belief that it's bad; that it's wrong; that it causes problems; and, of course, it does because you all *use* it instead of play with it. It is okay to love and it is okay to have sex with whoever is willing. If a small child is stimulated to the point that they wish for more, they are not guilty. Even you believe this much.

My pen cried that at five she enjoyed it and "let" him do it. It's her fault now in her mind; and what is her fault? It's her fault that she experienced release because an adult stimulated her as a child. So what? If you touch one another it feels good...... so what? Big deal. Please stop believing all this nonsense. You are spirit and soul enjoying the use of matter. You have created this suit that you wear and you may enjoy it in any way that you wish.

You may wish to know that my pen does not wish me to write on this subject as she still has concern and confusion regarding sexual abuse. I am working with her to release all fears and especially the guilt that she carries. Once again I will remind you that she is you. She has your problems in life and your confusions and even your pain. You are all confused on this subject and we must begin to clear this trauma for it is creating darkness.

Knowledge is power and to give you this information will begin a change in the way sex is viewed. I do not wish you to discuss this with others who see it differently. Know that it is not your job to change the belief system of others. It is my job and I will do this as I go. I am not speaking to them right now... I *am* speaking to you. You – "the man in the mirror." This is who we are working on now. Not the guy at work or our neighbor. It's all up to you to change you, and in changing you, you affect *all*. I will now tell you once again that Liane does not write this information. Do not attack her if you are unhappy about this writing. Attack me if you know how. I will be waiting and I will listen and I may even speak to you and give you my rebuttal. Go in peace and *know* that I am God and you are God and love.

❧❧

You do not wish to be so alone as you are now. Most of you do not know how to share love. You *use* your sex and you use one another. You will wish to learn to love from spirit which will give you a sense of giving and sharing and caring. You want so badly to be loved and to belong that you create situations for yourselves that are uncomfortable. You compromise and analyze and misunderstand what you receive.

You will wish to know that to love is to be exactly what you already are. Your natural state is love. Go with the flow and allow love. Love does not stop and analyze… "Oh he's not rich enough"… "Oops – this one's too short"… "Oh no – no hair" or "Just not my style." So, stop analyzing and judging and simply flow with what you first feel. Feelings are very important and you will wish to know that feelings and emotions are triggered by intuition which is the guidance mechanism of "higher self." So, listen to higher self. Wisdom is knowledge and to know how you function will allow you to know who you are. Do not be put off by the outside appearance. Go within to the heart and soul. Look for love and you will find love. Ask for love and I send love. You may not like what I have sent but you are receiving what is best for you now; this moment in time.

It is important to experience your fears in order to overcome fears. Fear is judgment. If he or she is too fat or too old or too skinny or too poor this is your fear showing. Go into this relationship until you no longer fear the situation. Each relationship has a lesson and each lesson is a gift. When you overcome your fears, you no longer draw what you fear. How can you learn to draw love when you are fear? Become love by letting go of fear. Fear leaves when we have taken a good look at it and decided that it's not so bad after all. So, if you do not wish to be with someone who is fat or skinny, maybe you should be with them until it no longer bothers you to be in this situation. You will learn a great deal and you will grow and you will change the way you see fat or skinny or rich or poor or just not attractive.

You do not judge from love. Know that when you find yourself saying "he or she is really interesting but…" this is judgment and 'fear of.' Go into fear and it fades away and you too will fade into love and draw what you most want. Until you are clear you will find it difficult to draw unconditional love because you are not unconditional. Now, for those of you who are married, I wish to explain that you too judge one another as not good enough or too fat or thin or old or immodest or slovenly and I wish you to stop judging and allow your partner to be. In allowing others to be you allow you to be. If he or she makes you crazy it is because you judge what he or she does, and when you begin to let go of these fear judgments then he or she will change because they have come to you to show you who you are and this was all agreed upon long ago.

Let go of this need to control. You spend your lives trying to make everyone into what you think is good and right and as you are learning in these books… you may not have all the right answers yourself. So let's just lighten up on one another and give the God inside a break. God is in everyone on this planet. Will you please let God tell you how to live and love. It is not so difficult. Please let me in. Do enema and allow me to show you who you are. You will have some confusion at first, but once the largest amounts of fear have left the body and subconscious, you will begin to not only see miracles, you will come to expect miracles.

I love you and I want to take care of you. I cannot without your permission. Stop putting me away from you. I have explained for Liane that I only want what is best for her, because what is best for her is best for me because I am her and she is me. Why in the name of heaven would I not "give" what God wants when I am God? Get out of the way and allow me to deliver your own good. God's good is waiting to come to each of you.

You must begin to clear fear. I will not clear for you. I will love you and I will guide you and I will tell you when you are judging and messing up, but I gave you free will and I cannot step in and change what you have created. I can only go where I am invited, and I am not allowed in because you are full already. There is no room for God. Your cup is full. Empty your bowels and allow the light in. Change your oil so we may run smoothly. I cannot do this for you. I am you and you must accept that I am who I say I am.

You are not to be so sure that you know what is best for God. Look around your world. Have you done what is best? You have done it your way so why not try God's way. What do you have to lose? Please give up and allow God to posses you. It's not so bad and the rewards will get better and better. You can be God instead of pain and confusion and distrust and unhappiness and unlovingness. You may pick up your pen and ask "why did this occur" and I will answer for you. I will not give you your answers as I do not wish to interfere with your learning, however I will guide you and tell you why you do not wish to be in your right place and I will tell you how to get to your right place; and I may even tell you things you do not wish to hear. Only I cannot tell you anything if you do not listen, and how can you listen if you do not believe that this is me – and of course that is a giant step for trust and faith. So, we are once again back to trust that I am God and the faith that allows trust.

God does not wish to trust for you, so you must do this one alone. Know that you do not wish to be alone and the quicker you choose trust the faster you develop faith, and with faith comes love and love is *all*. Absolutely everything comes with love... even miracles.

~ *Epilogue* ~

You do not wish to be "one" yet. You are so sure that you are separate from one another that you sit and watch and judge the person next to you, or the guy next door, or the neighboring nation. No nation is better than, and no planet is better than, and no world is better than. *Get this straight.* I am God and I am here to tell you to stop judgment. Stop telling others to fall to their knees and ask God's forgiveness, because God does not judge them as doing wrong. Stop begging to return to God because you already are God and you will return soon. You must learn to "be" exactly who you are at this time and to accept and love this you. I love you and I do not now nor have I ever judged and said you are wrong.

Now, for those of you who do not believe in God, you too wish to stop judging one another and begin to love you as the perfect being that you are. *There is no wrong.* Do not try to convince your neighbor of this and do not fling it in the face of your instructors, who are teaching you to live by their laws. You will learn in God's books how you are responsible for all that you do and you will also learn how you create your own reality. Do not judge what you have created as bad, because you have created it to learn by and it is not bad if you learn and grow.

So, now you are afraid you will run amuck and become mischievous and cause big problems for yourself, and I will show you how to be the best you can. Simply allow God in. Give me a chance; an opportunity to guide and direct and love and share in your life. You won't be asked to give up your wealth nor your fun. Continue to be you, but add to you by asking God to come into you and guide you. If you are a religious leader ask for my guidance again. If you are a gang leader ask for my leadership and I will come, and if you are a farmer ask for my power and it will be shown to you.

None is too great, none is too small. All, absolutely every person on this planet is part of God and therefore in touch with God. Not just the one who says that he speaks with me daily... all of you speak with me. You think and I am your thought process. You ask in your mind or wish for, and I must require that wish or thought, to become reality. You are literally your thoughts and you are thinking very dangerous thoughts. You think hate and anger and revenge, and these thoughts come back at you, and you are destroying you with your own painful thought process. Stop *judgment... you are judging you to death!*

Now, I do not wish you to believe that you do not wish to change. You do, and you each will. It is important at this time that you learn to be exactly who you are, because you are God, and to allow you to be is to allow God to be. You see, you are the only one in here. You are within this vast God force and you don't even realize that you are. So now you are growing and separating more and more, and you hate one another and he is part of you. And so the gang member who kills his hated rival is actually killing his own self, one limb at a time.

Please stop until I can show you who you are. You are harming you and I want to save you from self-destruction. You – not me – not the guy next to you – you! You are the one who has been guided by me to buy this book, or read this book, and it is no mistake. You are the one who can change what will happen in the lives of millions just by changing you. You are the only person on this planet and you are creating all this pain. And when you wake up to this fact, you will no longer wish to see life as you now do and all will change. No big mass movement, no protest, simply an awakening of you, by you. You are one person in this giant body called God and God wishes to wake up you and allow you to return home to him. It's time you know who you are and why God keeps sending word to you for such a long time.

It is no accident that Christ and Buddha taught my word. I have sent others and they too have been worshipped and turned into Gods. I am now writing to you so you will not follow another teacher. I figure it will be difficult to worship my books; however, you did a good job of worshipping the Bible, so who knows what you might make these into. Do not follow false Gods. Follow me. I am inside of you, and around you, and I am waiting to wake you up. I don't want your money. I don't want you to don robes and I don't want you to give up your lifestyle. I want you to laugh and sing and dance and love. Is that so dangerous? Is that so bad? How can you not agree with these fun ways of expression? How can you not see the good in becoming God?

Run and hide if you must, but I will still be here when you come out of hiding. I am not going away because I am your body and you are my body. You are inside the body of God and you are his blood and his cells, and you believe you are not special. You are the most special of all, because you are the only creation here. *You* did it all. You made it and you live in it, and because you see two of you, or three, or three million, does not mean you are more than one. You simply do not sit in a position to see the connection. You are all connected. One big body that is you and you are God's twin, and God wishes his twin to come home so that he can be whole. Father God is seeking out Mother God so he may put himself back together. This is how we will all wish to return... as one.

So, don't forget to think good thoughts about you, and you too will become good. Our next book will be called *The Neverending Love of God* and Liane looks forward to writing for you again. Say "I love you" to those you love, and hug yourself, because you are God and I wish to hug myself, only you must be my arms and my legs and my eyes. Open God's eyes and look... really look at who you are.

God

God's Pen

I first heard the voice of God in 1988. I was sitting in my back yard reading a book when this big booming voice interrupted with, "I am God and I will not come to you by any other name." I felt like the voice was everywhere – inside of me as well as in the sky around me. I was so frightened that I ran in my bedroom to hide.

This was not the first time that I heard voices. I had been communicating with my own spirit guide or soul for about a year. I guess my depth of fear regarding God, and all that he represented to me at the time, was just too much.

I spent two days trying to avoid the voice of God, which was patiently waiting for me to respond. By the second day I was exhausted from lack of sleep and decided to give in and talk with him. This turned out to be the greatest gift and best decision of my life.

The first book, *God Spoke through Me to Tell You to Speak to Him*, shows my evolution from communicating with my soul to communicating with the Big Guy. It took a couple years for me to be comfortable communicating with God. My fear of a punishing God was big! That has most definitely changed and I now think of God as my partner and best friend.

In the beginning the voice of God would wake me in the middle of the night and tell me it was time to write. He said I had promised to do this work (I assumed he was talking about the soul/spirit me). I would drag myself up to a sitting position and watch in amazement as my hand flew across the page, while I tried to keep up by reading what was being written.

It was always so much fun to wake up the next morning and grab my notebook to see what God had written during the night. After some time the voice stopped waking me and I became comfortable picking up my pen and writing for God first thing in the morning. I think in the beginning I had to be awakened while still semi-conscious from sleep so I wouldn't object too much to the information that was being channeled through me.

As I grew less and less afraid (and more trusting) of God, he was able to communicate greater information. Some of the information is quit controversial, but I felt it important to just let it be and not censor it. I present the writings here to you as they were given to me. I have edited a little (mostly the more personal information regarding myself) and I have used a pen name for privacy reasons. I asked God for a good pen name and he guided me to Liane which (I was told) in Hebrew means "God has answered."

At one point I became a little concerned about my sanity in all this, so I went to a hypnotherapist to find out what I was doing. Under hypnosis I saw this incredibly huge beam of light with a voice coming from within it. It was a giant "loving light" and felt so comforting and kind. It felt like that's where I came from. After that I stopped worrying about my sanity. If this is crazy, I think it's a very good kind of crazy to be....

In loving light, Liane

Loving Light Books

Available at:
Loving Light Books: www.lovinglightbooks.com
Amazon: www.amazon.com
Barnes & Noble: www.barnesandnoble.com

Also Available on Request at Local Bookstores